The Jewish War Against the Jews

REFLECTIONS ON GOLAH, SHOAH, AND TORAH

The Jewish War Against the Jews

REFLECTIONS ON GOLAH, SHOAH, AND TORAH

by

JACOB NEUSNER

KTAV PUBLISHING HOUSE, INC.
NEW YORK

BRESCIA COLLEGE
LIBRARY

51102

COPYRIGHT © 1984
JACOB NEUSNER

Library of Congress Cataloging in Publication Data

Neusner, Jacob, 1932-
    The Jewish war against the Jews.

    Includes index.
    1. Jews—United States—Identity—Addresses, essays,
lectures. 2. Jews—Diaspora—Addresses, essays, lectures.
3. Holocaust, Jewish (1939-1945)—Addresses, essays,
lectures. 4. Israel and the Diaspora—Addresses, essays,
lectures. 5. United States—Ethnic relations—Addresses,
essays, lectures. I. Title.
E184.J5N664 1984   305.8'924'073   84-9657
ISBN 0-88125-050-3

MANUFACTURED IN THE UNITED STATES OF AMERICA

For

Seymour Rossel

a hero in the struggle
for Judaism in America

Contents

Preface

Golah is any place Jews live outside of the Land of Israel. *Galut* is the condition of living where you do not wholly belong. That is, Galut is life in exile from where, or what, you should be. The one is geographical, the other, existential. Even without Zionism and the Jewish state, from the viewpoint of Judaism, America would remain a Golah, as much as Babylonia in Talmudic times. Even in the astonishing age in which we thrive, the age of the fulfillment of Zionism and the State of Israel, the condition of Galut endures, not limited by national frontiers.

I am three things, but logic dictates I should be only two of them: American, Jew, Zionist. You can combine the first and the second, or the second and third. But how to join all three in one person, living here? As a Zionist I affirm America—but as Golah, and myself as living in Galut. As an American, I can imagine no other place in which life is worth living. As a Jew I know how in a life of Torah to keep these other two convictions in uneasy balance.

This book presents reflections—essays, addresses—on the things I love and live for, this America, this Zion, this homeland in Torah expressed in a life of teaching about Judaism. It moves from the question to the answer. I begin with the question of America as Golah and a locus, among other places, of a life of Galut. I turn, second, to the principal evidence that we are not only in Golah but also subject to Galut. Third, I ask how we can bring Zion to our Golah and so claim to be those

1

two things that hardly fit together from the perspective of Zionism: Golah and Zion. Finally, I explain how, as a believing Jew, I find home in this Golah and address the world in which I really live with words framed out of my deepest convictions as a Jew, that is, speak words of Torah in Golah. That is the sum and substance of this book—love letters, statements from the heart, passionate expressions of caring.

The thesis of this book is that we American and Canadian Jews live in a paradoxical and dissonant world, because we affirm not merely Judaism but also Zionism. The resolution of the tensions between where we are and what we believe we are finds resolution in Judaism, that is, in the life in accord with Torah. Before proceeding to the particularities of our situation, therefore, I wish to explain why and how it comes about that Judaism in general imposes upon us the paradoxical consciousness and contradictory circumstance of conscience in which we live. For, in point of fact, our situation as Jews in Golah did not begin with us. It is natural to the definition of who the Jews are, where they should be, that emerges from the Torah itself. Since the Torah turns out to define us in so paradoxical a way, we have reason to ask the Torah to sort out the paradoxes and resolve the points of tension.

Why is it, then, that Judaism sees us as in exile? Where are we supposed to be, in line with the theory of the Torah, and how are we supposed to get there? Whence the contradictions of our condition?

Judaism focuses upon a particular place, but from the standpoint of nowhere in particular. It is locative in the setting of utopia. The enduring paradox flows from the peculiar circumstance in which the definitive documents of Judaism took shape. The Hexateuch—the five books of Moses and Joshua—as well as the principal historical books of the Scriptures—Judges, Samuel, and Kings, and the prophetic collections—all reached their final closure outside of the Land of Israel and in consequence of the loss of the Land to Israel. This formation of the Torah books took place in Babylonia after 500 B.C.E. All eyes then turn to Jerusalem, but from foreign land. The greater part of biblical literature therefore comes to us from writers bearing full knowledge of the loss of the Land of Israel—and its miraculous recovery. No wonder, then, that the Land should stand as a principal mark of the covenant between God and Israel.

The other Torah, the oral one, moreover, reaches its fulfillment in the Babylonian Talmud and shapes the law of Judaism in complete awareness of a Land once held, then lost, and always sorely missed. Accordingly, the yearning for the Land speaks out of the heart of exiles. Judaism as we have known it imagines one place at its center, while framing life for Israel, the Jewish people, wherever Israel endures, so, as I said, a locative religion coming from utopia.

If the ambiguous circumstance of the exile dreaming of home accounts for the paradox of a utopian-locative Judaism, the Babylonian Talmud, for its part, knows no doubt that one may practice its holy way of life anywhere, anytime. The issues of the kind of Judaism founded upon that document concern the sanctification of Israel wherever we may be: personal status, commercial transactions, the passing of the seasons. The system finds ample place for the Temple, hence for the holy city and the cult, to be sure, since, for the sages of the Babylonian Talmud, the return to Zion and the rebuilding of Jerusalem comprise the center of the symbolism of the messianic hope. There was no reason to leave such matters out. They contained no ambiguity about the present and served full well to join the messianic hope to the rabbinical discipline: Do this, so that will come about. Indeed, rabbinical Judaism is inconceivable without the messianic hope, hence without the full repertoire of Land-centered symbols. But the Babylonian Talmudic sages nonetheless managed to bypass the critical issue of Land, by omitting from their program of study—hence, the tractates they created—all attention to what, in the foundation-document, the Mishnah, fully expresses and exposes the Land-centeredness of Judaism.

It is in law, beginning with Scripture and proceeding to the Mishnah, that Judaism fully exposes its theology. The theology of the Mishnah, upon which the Babylonian Talmud rests, is a one-sided one, in which Israel can be Israel only in the Land of Israel. That position is expressed in two fundamental components of the six divisions of the Mishnah. In the view of the massive legal system on the subject of cultic cleanness, the Mishnah's sixth and largest division (about 26 percent of the whole in volume), one simply cannot attain cultic cleanness outside of the Land of Israel. All foreign land is by definition unclean with corpse-uncleanness. Accordingly, someone located outside of the Land of Israel is as if he were dead, so far as the system of cultic cleanness is concerned. Death is beyond the frontiers, life is within. The Babylonian Talmud ignores the whole of the Mishnah's repertoire of laws on cultic cleanness, except for the one on woman's menstrual uncleanness, pertinent anywhere Israel might find itself.

In the case of the equally critical legal system on the subject of Israel's obligation to God for its sustenance through the Land, the Mishnah's first division, on Agriculture, the message is equally clear. Israel holds the Land of Israel only as tenant; God is the landlord. Israel must hand over rations designated by God for his servants, the priests, and other parts of the produce of the Land, a rental fee or sacred tax owed to God for use of God's land (the view of Lev. 27:30). The point at which Israel becomes liable to pay this rent is the moment at which the farmer proposes to take for his own use the crops he has raised. In his study of Mishnah-tractate Maaserot, the fundamental statement on this matter, Martin Jaffee says, "God's claims against the Land's produce . . . are . . . reflexes of those very claims on the part of Israelite farmers. God's interest in his share of the harvest is first provoked by the desire of the farmer for the ripened fruit of his labor. His claim to that fruit . . . becomes binding only when the farmer makes ready to claim his own rights to its use." The point then is simple: for the Mishnah, to be Israel and holy is to live in the Land and to share in its bounty with God, the owner, in a relationship of mutuality and reciprocity.

How does the Babylonian Talmud deal with these stunning

and fundamental assertions of what it means to be Israel? The Mishnah's view, in the cited divisions, is locative: Israel lives only in the Holy Land. What it means to be Israel is to live life within the same framework of possession and emotion as God. The Babylonian Talmud, which is utopian, ignores both divisions entirely. It turns the Mishnah as a whole into something quite different, serviceable everywhere in general, restricted to nowhere in particular. So we can live Jewish lives all over.

The upshot is that when Israel in exile formed its fundamental vision of itself, it saw exile and redemption as the poles of its existence; life was lived within the tension of a yearning for some one place, in the hearts and minds of a utopian nation. At the same time, whenever the view from the Land became uppermost, the exiles managed to dispose of the claim that Israel could be Israel only in the Land (and State) of Israel by ignoring it. The great sages of Babylonia transmitted the Mishnah without commenting on its definitive divisions on Agriculture and Cleanness, turning it into something serviceable for the Golah. American Jews of our own day, confronted once again with the claim that normality is to live in the Land and abnormality abroad, authenticity is to be in Tel Aviv, inauthenticity anywhere else, do precisely what they want. They concede it all—amiably and even professing feelings of remorse and guilt—but in the English language, composed on the other side of the world from Jerusalem. If there is anything normative in the locative aspect of Judaism, it is in the never-to-be-resolved tensions, always chronic, today acute, imposed upon the existence and imagination of us, the Jewish nation.

We come to ourselves, here and now. These papers originally spoke for themselves. Here they will again. Let me simply explain how they are put together into a single, unraveling skein of discourse.

The prologue defines the setting for the entire book. In it I outline the program some of us set for ourselves nearly thirty years ago, in the 1950s, a program of the reform and renewal of the American Jewish community. In those quiet days we did not issue proclamations or take up picket signs. We talked among ourselves and set to work. I think we outlasted some who came after us; we certainly have survived our enemies.

We wanted the Jews to be more Jewish, in several specific ways. First, we missed, within the organized life of Jewry, a sense of relationship and caring. The institutions of Jewry, including those of Judaism, seemed to us formal and cold. Second, we looked out on the Jewish world and discerned the two definitive events of the age, neither one of them in those days appreciated in American Jewry: the destruction of the Jews in Europe, the creation of the State of Israel. I discovered both of them first hand when, as a student at Oxford, I traveled in Germany and in the State of Israel. When I came home, no one knew what I was talking about. Few in those days had been to Jerusalem. The calamity in Europe elicited silent horror. So we wanted "Israel," the Jewish people, to mean, at the very least, "the State of Israel." We wanted the Jews at home to mourn, every day, for the ones who had died.

We wanted the institutions of Jewry to address themselves to our condition, different from other Americans because we were Jews. Above all, besieged as we were in classrooms with the question, "Why should I be Jewish?" we wanted to give answers. Now, more than a quarter of a century later, all these things have come about. So there is the prologue: we got what we wanted. How good is it? The rest of the book explores the painful answer to that question.

To me the affirmations of Zionism speak about how things really are. Accordingly, I find it necessary not to argue about them, but to try to come to grips with them. The first and most important statement of Zionism is that outside of Zion is exile, expressed in two words, as I said at the outset, Golah, a mere fact of geography, and Galut, a judgment of the human condition. The second paper explores the condition of Galut. The third then turns to the commonplace claim that American Jews live in "two cultures," meaning, one American, the other, Jewish. The fourth signals the thesis of the book as a whole: for Jews not in Zion, Torah is the only homeland.

I state this thesis in secular terms. It is Jewish learning and intellect that have made the difference between the American and Canadian Jewish communities, which are essentially self-sustaining, and all the other Golah communities in the world, which depend for their inner life nearly entirely on the sustenance deriving from the State of Israel. I speak, of course, of the realm of ideas. In the marketplace of the Jewish mind, we export much, import only a little. The balance now favors us in ways in which, when I was young, it did not. So if we endure, it is because of our engagement in Torah.

The fifth paper turns to a commonplace Zionist judgment of the life of Israel in Golah: we shall not endure. In this regard I reject the implacable judgment of Zionism that life in the Golah must end.

The papers in Part Two take up the single paramount theme of American Jewish consciousness over the past decade and a half, the destruction of the Jews of Europe, which we call, in Hebrew, *Shoah,* and in English, "the Holocaust." The focus of my interest is in the place assigned to the Shoah in explanations of who we are and what we do as Jews in North America. The centrality of the Shoah in Israeli civil religion proves congruent to the everyday life of Jews in the Jewish state. For us, the same emphasis seems to me dissonant. That is the argument of the sixth paper. In the seventh I try to place the emphasis upon the Shoah into the context of the life of American Jewry's fourth generation. The purpose then is to explain why here, why now, those dreadful events take on myth-making proportions, serve to make sense of ourselves and to tell our story too. What is needed, I argue in the seventh and eighth papers, is a search for a story that speaks not only to us, but also about us, a tale about our hopes, not only a refraction of our fears. No one can make up such a story. A new myth— that is an oxymoron. Nor can you invent culture, declare civilization this morning, make up a tradition, or create a soul. But it does no harm to reflect, over and over again, on our circumstances and their meaning.

The third set of papers turns to the issue of our status as

Zionists and our relationship to the State of Israel. The issue came to the fore in the early 1970s, when the right of American Zionists to regard themselves as authentic to the cause came under serious questioning. In that context I offered the reply that Zion is integral to Torah, and Torah is our homeland. We must be Zionists; we have no choice. It is because we are Jews that we claim no alternative to Zionism and can imagine none. The ninth paper spells out that simple affirmation. In the tenth and eleventh papers I turn to the difficult question of how we, as American and Zionist Jews, relate to the State of Israel. The tenth paper refers, once again, to the circumstances in which the issue was joined. The eleventh paper takes up where the eighth and ninth leave off. The twelfth came nearly a decade later and presents a fresh angle. In it I stress the simple fact that until American Jews work out a theory of who they are and what they are doing here, they will have little to contribute to a dialogue with Israeli Jews.

The myth—the tale of eternally present truth—of Holocaust and Redemption, the centrality of Jerusalem, the primacy of the State of Israel in world Jewry—these convictions accurately portray the imagined situation of the ordinary Jew in the State of Israel. They are the only kind of Zionism available today. I for one can conceive no other. But how are *we* to live within such a framework of understanding of the Jewish condition? For the reasons spelled out in Parts Two and Three, the condition of Golah and the situation of Galut define the circumstances of our lives as Jews.

Yet while we talk as if we accept that definition of ourselves, we live as though there never was a Shoah, as if the redemption represented by the State of Israel saves someone else, as if Jerusalem were merely another city, the State of Israel another place to visit—the Jews' Disneyland—and world Jewry an undifferentiated mass. As I stress, our Israeli friends throw their hands up in despair when they contemplate our unmindful affirmation of opposites. For their convictions they give up their lives. For ours, what do we do? The scandal, the disgrace of our community once lay in its deliberate works of de-

Judaization. For all the amazing rebirth of these past two and a half decades, I begin to suppose, we have changed only little.

The penultimate paper describes the setting in which the work goes forward. So I recognize that where I started is where I now am, the struggle is the same, the issues unchanged. What we have seen in these past thirty years constitute important changes, in all but in the mind and heart of Jewry. So much have we accomplished. So much remains to be done.

But we do not work alone, nor do we have to complete the work in a single generation. If God loves Israel, others will take up where we leave off. Since God loves Israel, we shall yet prevail—even over the frail heart and infirm soul and insufficient mind.

Jacob Neusner

July 28th, 1982
The eighth of Ab, 5742
My fiftieth birthday.

Acknowledgments

These papers originated in the following places. I thank the respective copyright holders for permission to reproduce them here.

1. "We've Won. So What": *Moment*, vol. 2, no. 9, September 1977, pp. 61–62.

2. "The Jewish Condition and Galut": Etan Levine, ed., *Diaspora. Exile and the Jewish Condition* (N.Y., 1983: Jason Gronson), pp. 271-282.

3. "Living in Two Cultures": *Response*, vol. 6, no. 3, Fall 1972, pp. 105–16.

4. "Why We Are Different": Previously unpublished.

5. "The Ever-Dying People": *Moment*, vol. 3, no. 10, October, 1978, pp. 62-64.

6. "Beyond Catastrophe, Before Redemption": *The Reconstructionist*, April 1980, pp. 7–12.

7. "After the Flood, After the Rainbow": *Moment*, vol. 3, no. 6, May 1978, pp. 11–16.

8. "Other Times, Other Places, Us": As "Wanted: A New Myth," *Moment*, vol. 5, no. 3, March 1980, pp. 34–36, 61.

9. "Can We Be Zionists?": *Hadassah Magazine*, September 1972, pp. 10–11, 31. Address at the 58th national convention of Hadassah, August 21, 1972.

10. "American Jewry and the State of Israel: Toward a Mature Relationship": *The Jewish Frontier*, June 1972, pp. 18–23.

11. " 'We' and 'They'—or One People?": *The Jewish Frontier*, March 1973, pp. 20–25.

12. "Understanding the Other: Israeli Views of Us, Our Views of Ourselves": Previously unpublished. Address for the Jewish Community Council of Greater Washington, June 16, 1981, in honor of Mordecai M. Kaplan's centennial birthday and of the twenty-fifth anniversary of Kaplan's *New Zionism*.

13. "The Jewish War against the Jews": Previously unpublished. The Morris Adler Memorial Lecture, March 3, 1981, at Congregation Shaarey Zedek, Southfield, Michigan.

14. "Where Do We Go from Here?": Previously unpublished.

Prologue

1. We've Won. So What?

We asked the federations to be instruments of Jewish survival, instead of engines of assimilationism, and they are.

We demanded that the U.J.A. build the Jewish loyalties of younger people, rather than relying on the Jewish loyalties of the older generation, and it does.

We looked for means of achieving meaningful social relationships within Jewish community structures, and, in my case, I called for the re-creation of the ancient *havurot*, which I translated, "fellowships." Lo, we have *havurot*, and some even call themselves "fellowships."

We wanted to see the Holocaust remembered, and so it is.

We sought to focus on Zionist perspectives as the center of Jewish community discourse, with the issue of Israel at the heart of our collective life. There it stands, at the very center.

We pleaded for the improvement of Jewish education and for attracting talented young people to careers in that field, for greatly increasing the support of Jewish education on the part of federations and welfare funds. We have been heard.

We wanted more help for Hillel. All over the country, federations take a hand in the revival and improvement of Hillel on the campuses.

We wanted Jewish learning to percolate upward to the
campuses. In virtually all important universities at which sizable numbers of Jewish students are located it is possible to
take many worthwhile courses in Jewish subjects.

Shall I continue?

The list is very long. Back in the 1950's, twenty years ago, a
handful of lonely voices, taking seriously the religious revival,
the "return of the third generation," yet concerned at the same
time with "the vanishing Jew," wanted the Jewish community
to become both Jewish and Judaic.

In those days we used to analyze the allocations of federations and demonstrate how the money of Jewry is used to
starve institutions and organizations which make Jews Jewish
and to support those which are non-sectarian. There were
jokes about the three religions of democracy: Catholicism,
Protestantism, and non-sectarianism. We appealed to the
memory of the Holocaust. We evoked the achievements of the
State of Israel. We called forth recognition of the meaning of
our own historical experience—Holocaust, rebuilding.

And they listened to us.

That is not to say any one of our small number was heard. It
is only that the things we repeated in articles in obscure places
and in important ones, in speeches in every Jewish setting,
began to make sense to many people. We were the first to say
what, in time, many would be glad to hear, what would, in
time, become an almost conventional wisdom.

I do not think we can be more of a *Jewish* Jewish community
than we are now. Obviously, we have yet much progress to
make along the paths we currently travel. But it is difficult to
think of any goal we envisioned twenty years ago which is not
by now part of the institutional routine of the organized Jewish
community. All the words we proposed as fighting slogans are
now clichés, because our slogans have become programs. Our
agendum has been adopted. Among the doers and makers of
Jewry, what to us was fresh and important has become the
norm—and even normal.

For two decades I have been a minor prophet of this Judaic

renaissance. And I find all that I have described above accurate—and disappointing and empty.

For I have the unhappy sense that the things I laid before all who would listen twenty years ago were not the right things. I have been a false prophet, and I know it now. What I prophesied and preached has come to pass, but what has come to pass is not really very important. The measure of true prophecy, we recall, is that what the true prophet says will be comes to be. These things which twenty years have brought into being are what I wanted them to be. But they do not mean what I thought they would mean.

How so?

I have a sense that we have come just about as far as an ideology of Jewishness-as-survival can take us. There are large gaps in our inner lives as Jews which are yet to be filled. And all of the positive programs and policies have not really attended to those inner questions which await attention.

What I have in mind is not complicated. I am moved by the renewal of Jewishness and the resurgence, even, of Judaism. But why do I feel a sense of distance and emptiness, incompletion, when I should perceive fulfillment? We did not want to be the last Jews on earth—in North America, at least—and we are not. We have won. But what have we won?

What does it mean to us to be Jews and part of a continuity of Jews? When we have done our Jewish thing, how are we changed? How are we deeper people and wiser people? How are our lives more serene, our inner being more whole and complete?

We asked, and we were answered. But did we ask the right question?

Now that we have done all that we can do to insure our endurance as a distinct and distinctive people on earth, *so what?* What is it that we want to sustain and why?

I have spent my scholarly life asking these questions of the most influential period and document in the history of Judaism. The period is Judaism in late antiquity, from the destruction of the Second Temple to the rise of Islam; the document is the Talmud. What is it all about in that terribly critical time and place? What is the meaning, in its setting, of that extraordinarily influential document?

As I reflect on the work of nearly two decades, I find in it some continuing themes, of which the most important is this: How is it that the inner life, the life of the mind and of people learning, should have come to the fore as the single most important (though not the only) expression of piety and faith in Judaism? Why is it that Moses should be described as a rabbi, a man who learns Torah? Why is it that God should be portrayed as a master—not merely revealer—of Torah, and that the angels in heaven should be described as disciples of Torah?

Consider that the first seven centuries of our era saw the rise of the three great religions of the West: Christianity, Islam, and the form of Judaism we have known. Keep in mind that, in this same period, the great and orderly polity of antiquity came to an end. Then you realize that it was in a time of revolutionary change that the classical definitions of what we want to sustain and the reasons for sustaining it took shape.

For Judaism not only says that the Jews should continue as a distinctive group. Its holy books also say *why* they should do so, and, still more important, *what* they should do as an enduring people. Now I do not suggest for one minute that the next stage in our collective adventure in North America consists of building more yeshivas or (among the modernists, like myself) going off and getting Ph.D.'s in Judaic studies. I am only pointing out that there must be more of an answer than we have yet found to the question of what we do when we have succeeded in securing a fair measure of continuity.

I remember in the 1950's and 1960's the one question I would hear wherever I lectured was, "Why should I be Jewish?" I don't hear that question anymore. I suspect the reason is that those who wanted out have gotten out. I should guess that the intermarriage rate will now level off and perhaps even decline slightly. But I wish I now might hear the question, "Now that we are Jewish and plan to stay that way, *so what?*"

It is to answer that question that Judaic scholarship in all its forms, historical, theological, literary, is brought into being. I could not tell people why they should be Jewish, but somehow, it is clear, they know the answer. But I should be able to tell people what lay at the center and heart of Jewish existence for times past, and even suggest what may find a place in the heart and soul of Jewry now.

For I perceive, in all this success, this resurgent Jewishness and even rediscovered Judaism, an inner space, an emptiness that cannot and should not be filled solely by saving Soviet Jews, remembering the Holocaust and learning from it, making pilgrimages to the State of Israel, working for the federations, even by regular participation in synagogue life.

The ideology of peoplehood-and-history, whether expressed in fund drives or in classrooms, calls forth the giving of money and the learning of historical facts. That ideology is necessary. Its effects are laudable. And it is insufficient.

I am not sorry that we no longer ask, "Why be Jewish?" In seeking to answer that question, we stumbled across ways of Jewishness that satisfied, for a time; learning how to be Jewish, asking "why" became pointless. Now it is time for us to ask the next question, and to pursue the next answer: for what? How shall we remember and invent a Judaism that speaks not only to the necessity of survival of this great historic people, but that speaks also to the compelling needs of each individual Jew, of each of us who searches for meaning, for life, for understanding, for self?

Part One

Golah Without Galut?

2. The Jewish Condition and Galut

The State of Israel has ended the political exile of the entire Jewish people, wherever they live, wherever they are, the Jews are there by choice. No Jew needs to be a refugee. So far as Galut stands for being homeless or where one does not wish to be, that sort of Galut has ended. What is left of the idea of exile, however, is a rich and evocative picture of the human situation. For Galut may have been principally a political condition. But it never was only that. Today, as I said, it is not that at all. It is once more a symbol for the condition of the world in its flawed relationship to the Creator of all life. So far as Galut is deemed a locative category, describing where one is, it is no longer relevant to the life of the Jewish people. So far as Galut is understood as utopian and existential, an account of alienation, then we deal with a vivid and provative mode of insight.

Exile and the Jewish Condition

Galut as an approach to the interpretation of American Judaism is politically irrelevant, socially pernicious, economically dysfunctional, religiously meretricious, but essentially correct. For Galut speaks of alienation, disintegration, and inner strife. American Jews politically, socially, and economically stand within the corporate limits of society; they do not see themselves as temporary residents, people who really belong somewhere else. Their homeland is America; its turmoil is theirs; so too is tragedy and triumph. To allege that in the eschaton they will magically be lifted up and transported on eagles' wings to some other place is to present American Jews with a useless fantasy. One might as well tell them stories of Sinbad the sailor and call them theology, or history.

But speak of alienation and one addresses the center of the Jewish situation. American Jews are in Galut, exiled from the joys and glories of Torah. They have lost the art of dying, the public pleasure of celebration together, the glory of a day of rest together, the splendor of perpetual awareness of the natural cycle, above all, the capacity for atonement and the certainty of forgiveness. They have no shared myth within which to explore life's private mysteries, through which to locate the meaning of public events and of felt history. Their mythic life is insufficient. Their most abysmal exile of all, therefore, is from the human quest for meaning.

The existential dimension of Galut encompasses the situation of American Jews as modern people. Having lost the capacity unselfconsciously to participate in tradition, the modern Jews—whether here or in the State of Israel—find themselves lost and virtually helpless. They cannot go backwards, but see no way forward. The insights of tradition into the human condition, while sound and perpetually correct, come in symbols to which they cannot respond, garbed as absolutes to which they cannot submit. So they pathetically limp from cause to cause, drawn in the currents of searching humanity, from one headline to the next. This is the contemporary counterpart to the wandering of the Jewish people from land to land, the former incapacity of Jewry ever truly to settle down. Political Galut is a paradigm for the existential Galut of our own time. And both mirror a deeper side to the human heart—the soul's incapacity ever fully to accept, to love, not only the other, but, to begin with, the self. If in former times the collectivity of Israel saw itself as alien to its situation but at home in its religious community, today nearly the whole Jewish people has exchanged political Galut for one that is more comfortable and secure, if in a measure also self-pitying and narcissistic: alienation from the art of living.

But these reflections on Galut have carried us far from the accepted range of discussion. Let me give blunt answers to the questions on the conventional agenda.

The traditional concept of Galut, phrased in either historical, political, or metaphysical-Kabbalistic terms, does not and cannot characterize American Jewry. It would be pretentious to elevate the banal affairs of a bored, and boring, ethnic group, unsure of its identity and unclear about its collective purpose and meaning, to a datum of either metaphysical or even merely historical hermeneutics. American Jewry simply does not add up to much. Its inner life is empty, its public life decadent. So to whom shall we ask the ultimate questions of meaning? To what shall we apply the transcendent symbols of exile and alienation? To Bar Mitzvah factories and bowling clubs? It would be not merely incongruous but derisive.

At home in American or Western civilization? Alas, as much at home as anyone. Why abstract ourselves from the generality of people in general? What choices do we have? In all the world, who aspires to something other than our civilization, our way of living? Shall we repudiate jet planes or penicillin or liberal democracy? For what? The oxcart, the medicine man, and the messianic general? These hardly improve the human condition.

And if we were to migrate to the State of Israel, what gain should we hope for? To be a Jew in America is no harder than to be an American in Israel, but whichever one is, he or she remains in the situation of exile. Only propagandists seriously ask us to interpret Galut so crassly that its effects may be washed away by a trip across the oceans. No baptism there, nor a new birth in a new world. The new creation, new heavens, and new earth—these are harder to attain.

It follows that Jews whether at home or in the State of Israel cannot repudiate their millennial history of Galut any more than they repudiate their truncated history of "enlandise-ment." Having, and not having, a land of our "own"—both are integral to the Jewish experience of history. The felt history of the Jewish people is single, unitary, integrated: the experience of one people in many places and circumstances, not one of

them barren of meaning and insight. They all of them constitute the Jewish testimony on the history of mankind, with most
of which the Jews are coextensive. Shall we now be asked to
say that the lessons of the Land are true but the lessons of
Galut are false? Are not the great monuments of our spiritual
and intellectual history both in the Land and outside of it? And
do we not give up our responsibility to stand outside of and to
judge the history and works of mankind if we repudiate our
own creation within that history and among those works? And
that creation is in a measure the capacity to live as strangers at
home.

Galut has nothing to do with whether or not the Jews are
fully accepted "as human beings," for it is not created by the
world and cannot be changed by it. But for my part, if I am
accepted as a "human being" and not as a Jew, I do not accept
that acceptance. I aspire to no place in an undifferentiated
humanity and hope never to see the end of significant differences among people and peoples. The only "acceptance"
worth having is of myself as I am, first, last, always a Jew, son
of my people as I am son of my father, and, I hope, progenitor
of Jews as well. Take me despite my Jewishness and there is
nothing to take. Overlook what is important to me and you
obliterate my being. Of that sort of acceptance we have had
enough in the liberal sector of American society. It has yielded
self-hatred and humiliation, and, for Jewry at large, an inauthentic existence. So acceptance of the Jews "fully as human
beings" not only intensifies but also poisons the awareness of
Galut. It denies to us our dignity, our loyalty, our right to be
ourselves.

Nor does anti-Semitism do much good, for exactly the same
reasons.

Granted, Galut ends with "the living of an authentic Jewish
existence," but that life is not to be defined by where it is lived.
What matters is how. By "authentic" and "Jewish" one may
mean many things. To me an authentic Jewish life is one of joy
and gladness, a life that fulfills the many-splendored hopes of
humanity with the light of Torah. And Torah illumines the

world, no one part more than another. American Jews will have attained an "authentic Jewish life" when they look forward to Sabbaths of contentment and festivals of rejoicing, when they celebrate natural glories and share the human pathos, when they have so educated themselves that whatever happens enters into Torah and also explains its meaning.

The end of our exile— and the exile of Jews wherever they may be—will come with the end of alienation, disintegration, and inner strife. On that distant day we shall be at one with ourselves, at one in society, and at one with God. We will know the joy of Torah in the private life and for the public interest, and Torah will open the way to God. And the first step on that long, long road is the start of the search for the joys of being Jewish—trivial, humble pleasures, such as welcoming the sunset on the eve of the Seventh Day and singing songs about the Lord, master of the world, rock of whose goodness we have eaten, the honored Day. Sung without belief, to be sure, but the song contains all the belief we need. Our voices, our words, our melodies—these resonate as one—the echo of our ultimate unity, the end of our exile from ourselves, the beginning of the inner peace we seek.

The Jewish Condition and the Human Condition

It is time, therefore, for the sons and daughters of the Golah to give up that dishonest pose of apology we have played out before our Israeli counterparts. Without apology or restraint they proclaim our faults: "You are disappearing through assimilation. Anyhow, the *goyim* are going to kill you all. So your destiny is to die in gas chambers, singing 'Silent Night.' " In utter silence we bypass theirs—and (out of embarrassment) refrain, too, from declaring what we believe we have to cherish in the experience of Galut.

But there have been lessons. The framers of radically locative Israelism, in which *only* being-Jewish in the State of Israel is "authentic," and being-Jewish anywhere else is "inauthentic," may well be reminded that we have learned lessons they have not learned. These lessons have the power to make us into significant exemplars of precisely that Judaism that is shared among us all. Let me therefore describe what I think being a Jew in the Golah has taught me—lessons Israelis might well attempt to learn as well.

The Jewish situation in the Golah endows me, first of all, with a long and formidable perspective. It forces me to see myself as part of a continuum of time and of space, as heir of some of the most sublime and most foolish men that have ever lived, and as friend and brother of people who, in days past, lived almost everywhere humanity has been. I cannot therefore accept provinciality, either temporal or spatial, or see myself as rooted forever in one culture or in one age.

Thus the Jewish situation in the Golah is international and cosmopolitan, and never wholly part of one place or time. This is both a blessing and a curse. It is a blessing because it assures me of ultimate detachment, of a capacity to contemplate from without, to think less fettered by rooted attachments than other people. It forces not only detachment, but to some measure, an act of selection and judgment also, for, not being fully committed anywhere or ever, I am forced to perceive what others may stand too close to see, and in perception, to respond, to judge. I must therefore learn to love with open arms, to know that this land, this people are mine, yet not wholly so, for I belong to Another as well. Thus to be a Jew means in a historical and more than historical sense to be always homeless in space and in time, always aware of the precariousness of people, of the possibility, by no means remote, that I may have to find another place.

But the Jewish situation of homelessness, of detachment, has provided me, second, with the awareness that what is now is not necessarily what was, nor what must always be. Being able to stand apart because of an inherited and acquired perspective of distance, I realize the people have choices they may not themselves perceive, that there have been and are now other ways of conducting life and living with others, of building society and creating culture, than those we think are normative. Being able to criticize from the perspective of other ages and lands, I am enabled to evaluate what others may take for granted, to see the given as something to be criticized and elevated.

Third, the Jewish situation of living with a long perspective imposes upon me a terrible need to find something meaningful, truly eternal in human affairs. If I see that all things change, and that only change is permanent, then I need all the more a sense of what abides in humanity, of what endures in human civilization. If one says, with Sinclair Lewis's men of Gopher Prairie, that to build the emporium that is ours, Washington weathered the rigors of Valley Forge, Caesar crossed the Rubicon, and Henry stood at Agincourt, then one declares faith that what is here is truly the Zenith and the end of Western history. But we Jews know differently, for we know of cities once great and now no more, of civilizations—and we too have built civilizations—that prospered and were wiped out in time. We ask, therefore, because we need to ask: what abides, what is permanently meaningful in life? We want to know where history is moving, because we know that history does, indeed, move.

Fourth, out of this need, this thirst for meaning in kaleidoscopic life, we Jews have learned that something in humanity is indeed eternal. We use the words of Scripture, and say that "humanity is made in the image of God," but underlying these words is a mute and unarticulated awareness that humanity prevails, and some achievements can endure. We know, moreover, what will live, namely, the intellect, the capacity to learn. We have, therefore, dedicated our best energies to the cultivation of the mind, to study, enrichment, and transmission of humanity's insights and ideas through the ages. We have held that that part of humankind which may think, know, believe, hope, love—that part is divine and endures, and whatever part of it endures from another age is ours to know, love, and cherish. Therefore, in other ages, our monuments have been books, the schoolhouse, and our heroes have been people of learning and of mind.

Fifth, because I am a Jew, I understand how important to the world are compassion and our capacity to transcend the animal base through acts of love and fellowship. The Jewish situation imposes this understanding in two ways.

Because we were slaves in Egypt, we know how important is an act freely done, freely given, that at its most elevated is represented by compassion. Because we have suffered in history, we have learned how important is the opposite of cruelty and oppression, namely, kindness and love.

Because we see ourselves as human, neither animals nor God, neither wholly objects of nature and history nor wholly subjects of nature and history, we see our human duties and capacities as neither wholly passive nor on the other hand entirely active. We know, therefore, that we may *do* little, but that we may *do:* and what we may do as an act of our own will is to act decently, compassionately, justly, for free will permits us to choose compassion. The larger part of life may be "conditioned," and outside of our power, but that precious corner of freedom to act by one's own will remains, and *will* at its most virtuous is goodwill, in Hebrew *hesed* (in the abstract, compassion) and *gemilut hasadim* (in the concrete, acts of compassion).

Sixth, more concretely, the Jewish situation imposes upon me an intensity of human relationship, best embodied in the family and people, that others see as clannishness. Seeing the world as we do, a lonely, insecure, transitory place, we look within it for places of security and evidences of permanence, and these we find, as I said, in the abstract in compassion, and in the concrete, in human relationships of love and deep acceptance. We know that death is always near, and that each one goes a separate way to death. But we find in this knowledge not only separateness, but also union of the generations. Death is the experience that brings together the generations that have gone before and those that will come; it is the one experience we share in common. God's power and will abide to unite the generations. This is the source of veneration of our past and our capacity continually to live in it, and the foundation of our love for our people, wherever and whenever they are found.

Finally, the Jewish situation has as its foundation a continuing confrontation with the reality of God. Until now, one may have wondered where is the theology of the Jewish situation. Beyond the theologies of Jewish religion, and before them all, is the simple sentence, "In the beginning God created the heaven and the earth." That is our fundamental affirmation, and all else must be built on that fact. We affirm that God, who made the world, did so purposefully, and ultimately that purpose is revealed in the course of human history. All that I have said about our long and formidable perspective, our awareness of the frailty and transitory quality of man, our thirst for permanence, through dedication to the mind and reason, to love and compassion in the abstract and in concrete terms—all this is founded upon our fundamental attitude toward the world and ourselves, both of which we see to be the objects of divine concern, divine purpose, divine compassion. Both humankind and nature are objects, not subjects, of reality, both are profane, and the only sanctity lies beyond the world and humankind. Hence our concern for history and its movement, for humanity and conduct in society arise out of our awareness that in the objects of creation we see in pale reflection a shadow of the Subject.

Because of this awareness, we are not ashamed of our history, of our frailty and inconsequentiality as a small and insignificant people among the peoples of mankind. We know that those great nations that ruled the world like God perished like all mortals, while we who have patiently endured in hope endure today. Therefore we do not reject our tragic past.

Very little has been said here to distinguish Jews from other men. It is hardly necessary to be a Jew to understand the Jewish situation. The existential qualities I have described are those that Jews may know best and longest, but others know them too. We have words for our situation, such as *Galut*, exile, *Rachmanut*, compassion, *Yosher*, righteousness, and *Bitahon*, faith, trust in God; and these words, though ultimately not translatable into any other language, are in fact shared existentially by every other people today.

An age that is threatened by the total destruction of entire civilizations knows what it means to be Jews, who suffered the destruction of their entire European civilization in our time. An age that knows no security knows what it means to be Jews, who have lived for thousands of years without security. An age that finds itself almost powerless to change the course of history, in which individuals find they are almost impotent to affect events, knows what it means to be Jews, who have lived as outsiders, standing always on the wings of history and never in the spotlight. An age that suddenly realizes it is in the grip of past events knows what it means to be Jews, who have seen themselves forever in the grip of events they have not caused, and ultimately, in the hand of Providence. An age that now knows the danger of nationalism and provinciality knows what it means to be Jews, who have lived internationally before there were nations.

If this is so, perhaps others will learn from us the affirmative lessons of our situation: our quest for meaning in events, our consecration to the human intellect and capacity to think, to create and preserve culture; our appreciation of the preciousness and sanctity of humanity's slender treasure of compassion and of love, in the abstract and also in day-to-day human relations in which, after all, we do retain considerable power; and, finally, our awareness of the reality, immediacy, and centrality of God's will, our knowledge that in the end, it is not we but God who determines the history of individuals and nations, not with ourselves but God with whom we must strive for blessing.

3. Living in Two Cultures?

The view that American Jews live in two cultures, or 'civilizations,' was pertinent to the situation of the children of immigrants. To them, "Jewish culture" was a "thing," clearly defined in terms of language, social and cultural context, and values. Their unitary and one-dimensional view of "Jewish culture"—the Yiddish culture of their parents—was possible because they stood on its fringes and could perceive the alien character of the parents' world. But the children of immigrants envisaged American culture, to which they were marginal, likewise as a unitary phenomenon. Their horizons were limited, after all, to their neighborhood, which was apt to be Jewish, and their job, which was situated within a narrow slot of urban American life. They had little perception of the richness and diversity of the country; they had slight opportunity to get to know it. They faced a world only partially open; if they went to college, it was to a local school, where they met people like themselves, also the children of immigrants, also marginal to the larger America beyond the local setting. So for the second generation, both "Jewish culture" and "America" could be regarded as simple "things" and apprehended—on both sides—as somewhat foreign.

The third and later generations of American Jews do not live in "two cultures." The concept is irrelevant to their situation. The Jews they know as models speak English, are university graduates, make a living in a wide range of professions and businesses, and in mode of life and values are not sharply

31

differentiated from non-Jews. American Jews have no special language, no special politics, no unique patterns of human relationships, nor do they form a well-defined sub-culture in American life, except for certain relatively trivial cultural and, at times, religious practices and for a commitment to endogamy and to Israelism. These things do not add up to a "culture"; they are at best a highly particular mode of middle class life. One can hardly claim American Jews in the mass preserve so different a view of life and its meaning, so unique a concept of ethics and morality, so special a concern for their own cultural and religious traditions, as to constitute a unique "culture" in the way that Chicanos, or Blacks, or Polish- or Italian-Americans still do. Their ideals are not much different from those of upper-class Protestants; as a social group they tend to conform to the model of (for New England) the Yankees. At the same time they know too much about America to conceive of their homeland as consisting of a single "culture." They perceive of the immense regional, social, and especially, class differences in American "culture." Having chosen for their assimilatory model the sub-division of upper-class Protestants, they are quite well aware that to be "American," they do not have to model their lives and values after other available models.

The definition of "Jewish culture" fails because the data on the Jews in various places and times hardly permit a unitary conception of "the Jewish people." Speaking in a secular way, one may refer only to various groups called "Jewish," an adjective bearing various meanings in diverse settings and serving particular functions within different societies, past and present. To one outside the theological or ideological framework of Jewish belief, the "Jews" as a group are best defined functionally and episodically, not normatively. Consequently one cannot locate "Jewish culture," though clearly one may define Yiddish-Ashkenazic culture, from which American Jewry stems. Jewish "culture" is what is done, I suppose, when people born of a Jewish mother or converted to Judaism do things for reasons connected with being Jewish. True, people suppose there are religious or cultural or sociological traits characteristic of "the Jewish people" from remote antiquity to the present day. Such people would claim there is an "essence of Judaism," if they are religious, or some sort of quintessentially "Jewish" life-style, quality, or character to be observed in this worldly-terms, if they are secular. They are led into a kind of historicistic thinking; they do not, however, do good history, for their ideology prevents it.

We are left, in my opinion, with the classic Judaic religious tradition, which *can* be defined and studied, which does exhibit important, normative continuities from place to place and age to age. But the Judaic tradition is transnational; it can be authentically embodied within a diversity of cultural settings— languages, societies, economic structures. The Sabbath, for example, may be variously observed in fifth-century Pumbedita, twelfth-century Granada, nineteenth-century Koretz, or twentieth-century Providence. Its definition is one and singular; local customs will not obliterate the essential unity of the holy day. No one can doubt that the Judaic religious traditions can be and are being carried out in America, nor is there reason to suppose they have no meaning for the Jew within the diversity of American societies.

Clearly, the formation and development of Judaic religious life in America will alone define the American Jew and will uniquely make significant and impart meaning to his being separate, a Jew. The task is important not alone for the continuity of Jewish existence but also for the elevation of American social and cultural life. Judaism in its diverse formulations is needed by a society in search of cohesion, dignity, and a more than material purpose for life. For Judaism has shown the capacity to ennoble and sanctify the lives of ordinary people, to draw them together out of their private concerns and to make of them a society, a People. The Judaic tradition for centuries and under every circumstance has manifested the capacity normatively to define the Jewish condition. It is the Judaic tradition which speaks to the eternal issues of death and life's purpose, which asks questions about the meaning of existence and gives answers to those questions. The Judaic tradition imparts meaning to the anguish of the ordinary man and woman, gives transcendence to their life, lends purpose to their effort. It takes those ordinary persons and shows them to be part of an extraordinary People, links them to its past and assigns them a place in its destiny, grasps hold of their private time and personal life and joins both to the rhythm of eternity. Judaism links their mortal being to the natural course of the days and the seasons, just as it links their private being to the eternal existence of the People. Judaism has shown how to impart dignity to the affairs of the ordinary man and woman and cohesion to the affairs of the community and a higher purpose to the life of the community. A nation in search of itself can have worse than a holy community in its midst, as model and paradigm for its larger quest.

Obviously, a formidable task faces the American and Canadian Jews, therefore, for they stand far from the Judaic tradition of which I speak, and can scarcely claim that community life both is paradigmatic and supplies useful lessons for the larger society. The Jew is a kind of American; but Jewishness-Americanness bears little transcendent meaning. Today the Jew is trivial, and Jewishness a matter of superficial traits; we are marginal to Judaism. But that does not mean that tomorrow and beyond things must remain as they now are.

If, therefore, the Jew has anything to give to America or to Canada, it has to be through Judaism. Otherwise, we are uninteresting and banal. What we have to offer, however, we have first to take in to our own being. Spiritual greatness and a largeness of humanity depend upon both inner and the communal appropriation of, assimilation to, Judaism. It is, after all, Judaism which makes the Jewish-animal into a human being, and if the Jewish-animal does not attain humanity through Judaism, he or she is going to become human in some other mode, an unnatural and to them inauthentic one at best. If the Jews are to participate in American life as a perceptible type of American, it is through Judaism that we will be formed for worthy purposes.

It is, I contend, false to suppose that the Judaic tradition does not nurture the development of individuality—though admittedly, in its Orthodox forms, it stands against individuality; to regard the Judaic tradition as impoverished in respect to the imaginative life; to find barren its message regarding interpersonal relations, the unique role of women; to allege that Judaic living is impertinent to the life of the family; to hear no Judaic message about the moral use of power. As to the last, a people which has found a way to express hostility and aggression without force has much to say about the moral use of power. A people which has sustained itself through the richness of family life has resources for the reconstruction of the family. The careful and thoughtful definition of sexual roles and relations and the elevation through rational inquiry of interpersonal relations—these constitute one of the great themes of the Jewish law, and not only of the law. Imagination, insight, and individuality—have these not formed the center of the intellectual enterprise which for so long has occupied the Jewish people?

What is lacking is not in the tradition but in ourselves, above all in those who represent the tradition as smaller and less humane than it has always been. The tradition has too long been understood as the monopoly of the traditionalists, but the fault is not theirs. They alone were sufficiently loyal and devoted to being Jewish as to learn something of the heritage of Judaism. They were, alas, also not very "cultured," insufficiently educated to the task, parochial, narrow-minded, and obscurantist. But it was not Judaism that made them so, for in other times and other lands the formative spirits of Judaism were hardly parochial, narrow-minded, and obscurantist, but people of broad humanity, breadth of soul, and rationalist. The contemporary modes of creativity by and large stand alien to the exponents of contemporary Judaism; the people committed to "being Jewish" have yet to trouble to make themselves aware of the need for something beyond commitment: knowledge, deeply besought, profoundly assimilated. But the knowledge of which I speak is not historical or narrowly textual; merely knowing biblical or Talmudic literature, the facts and dates of Jewish history produces little more than learned barbarians. The sources are our resources. What we make of them is the measure of, not our Jewishness, but our humanity. We may indeed be altered by knowledge not at all. And we may think we know what we actually perceive merely as a slogan or as a fact. It is much, much harder to be a Jew than has as yet been perceived.

4. Why We Are Different

Of all of the Jewish communities of the Golah, only one sustains its inner life of culture and faith independent of Jerusalem—and only one can hope to. That community is the North American Jewish world of the United States and Canada. No other Golah community has the resources to maintain itself without a continuing infusion of Israeli cultural and spiritual assistance. Programs of sending teachers, youth leaders, and other builders of the community's future provide such day-to-day leadership as exists in the rest of the Golah. We produce our own teachers, rabbis, scholars, and other builders. That is the difference.

Obviously, we derive immense benefit from our Israeli connection too. In many ways we are better able than others to utilize to our own advantage the cultural datum of the Jewish state. For we can appropriate the Israeli part of the Jewish experience for our own purposes. We make use of the Jewish state as a vast language laboratory and as a living model of the varieties of Jewish existence. But we bring home what we learn for the enrichment of our community. Because we have the inner strength and autonomy, we adapt for our own use and circumstance what works well—but in different ways—in the State of Israel. Other Jewish communities have no choice but to turn themselves into miniature Israels, presenting in pretty much its Israeli form such cultural sustenance as they have to begin with. There is slight adaptation, because there is nothing to which to revise and adapt the Israeli component. So if you are going to be Jewish in the sense of reading Jewish books, engaging in Jewish cultural enterprise, thinking Jewish thoughts, making sense of your being as a Jew, you see yourself as a displaced Israeli—everywhere but here.

For we have our Jewish novelists and thinkers, our Jewish issues and arguments, our varieties of being a Jew, independent of those of the Jewish state. Our politics as a community takes shape independent of the politics of the State of Israel. Israeli political parties, competitive and powerful throughout the Golah, stand for little in North America. The vigor and vitality of our inner life as a community, its religious institutions, its schools, its programs for higher education of all kinds, its informal group life in all its complex and interesting variety—all of this sets us apart from the rest of the Golah. We present a problem to Jerusalem, because, in point of fact, to us Jerusalem is not that unique center of culture which it is for Johannesburg, Melbourne, Auckland, Buenos Aires, or London Jewries. Our Jewish life is strong and indigenous, in ways in which, elsewhere, it is not.

Now, as I said, the difference does not lie in numbers alone. There is a critical mass of Jews sufficient to sustain significant institutions of culture and faith. It must be so numerous as to produce students and teachers, so rich as to maintain institutions of education and culture, and so caring as to want to do so. Those three conditions, depend, I think, on a number of something in the order of 100,000–125,000 Jews. The reason I think so is that it is roughly the number of Jews which stands behind the Hebrew college systems of Boston, Cleveland and Baltimore. If communities of such a size can sustain teacher-training schools (and so much else), then we should expect to find equivalent institutions wherever there are Jews in such numbers. But, of course, we do not. There is a reason. The cultural ambitions of the North American Jewish community are not replicated in South Africa, Britain, France, Argentina, or Australia.

In every other way these communities compete with us. In philanthropy, in support of the State of Israel, and in other

ways we are not the equals of South African Jewry, for example. The moral courage of that Jewish community is not fully
understood overseas; we are not their equals. Yet South African Jewry is dull, sleepy, engaged in a protracted process of
quiet death, because it neither has nor wants Jewish life of the
spirit and soul. Its synagogues are formalistic; its rabbis in the
main tame and unambitious; its lay leadership actively hostile
to matters of culture and faith. British Jewry for its part is
famous for its dumb indifference to humanistic learning and
expression of Judaism. Its institutions of Jewish learning are
notorious for their mediocrity, and, on the average, so are their
graduates. From Australia nothing is heard. France would
appear to have produced five or six significant scholars of
Judaic studies, for its more than half-million Jews. By the same
standard, the State of Israel should have thirty-six—instead of
hundreds! So the picture is clear.

We therefore have to draw the simple consequence that the
single most important source of inner power in North American Jewry lies in its rabbis, teachers, professional scholars,
community "professionals" of all kinds. And what makes them
distinctive and effective is the education they bear, the vision
they receive and transmit. Under dreadful circumstances, Jewish educators maintain a high standard of purpose, even
though they cannot always attain it. Corroded by doubt and
ignorance, rabbis try to find something to say, from week to
week, which is relevant and consequential. Assaulted by indifference, the "professionals" carry on the workaday task of
drawing within the orbit of Jewry the larger number of Jews in
every city and town. If people are drawn to this Jewish labor
and are sustained in it, it is by a vision which has captured
them in their youth, by an education which has informed them
at the threshold of their active life.

It is time to acknowledge the centrality to North American
Jewry of those little Jerusalems among us; I mean the tottering
institutions of Jewish learning, from which the rabbis, teachers, and professionals go forth. Their flaws are obvious; I am
not alone in speaking of them in public. But if we see the flaws,

it is because we look. We look because we care. We care because we understand. If we are an essentially self-sustaining Jewish community in America and Canada, it is because we have institutions of mind to sustain us. Take away those institutions, however small, however weak, however struggling, and what is left is a formless mass, a huge replica of South African or British or Australian Jewry, vacant of all Jewish spirit except what is inherited from overseas, lacking all Jewish intellect—all form, no meaning, all money, no heart.

So let us praise them—it is fitting to do so—who make the difference: the teachers colleges, the day schools, high schools, seminaries, and yeshivas, the Jewish universities; the publishers, the magazine editors, the writers and intellectuals, philosophers, theologians, scholars; the journalists, the musicians, and the poets and the dancers and the sculptors and the artists and the dramatists and the novelists and the psychiatrists. Crackpots all—praise them all, those troublers of Israel's peace.

It was not for nothing that the Cambodian Communists killed anyone who wore glasses.

5. The Ever-Dying People

We are a people obsessed, and it is our own death that obsesses us. The great Jewish philosopher, Simon Rawidowicz, who died just two decades ago, gives us an important insight into ourselves when he says, "The world makes many images of Israel, but Israel makes only one image of itself, that of a being constantly on the verge of ceasing to be, of disappearing." This he says in his essay, "Israel, the Ever-Dying People." Our task, therefore, is to find a way of living with our own mortality, of accepting what cannot be changed, and of living out our destiny with dignity and maturity.

Rawidowicz spells this out: "He who studies Jewish history will readily discover that there was hardly a generation in the Diaspora period which did not consider itself the final link in Israel's chain. Each always saw before it the abyss ready to swallow it up. . . . Each generation grieved not only for itself but also for the great past which was going to disappear for ever, as well as for the future of unborn generations who would never see the light of day."

It is not hard to see how such a gloomy perspective has gripped our people. In our own time, for example, we need only look at the small Jewish communities to understand its development. In my own community, as in so many others, the Jews grow old, their children have moved to the larger cities, there is no vision, there is no leadership, there is no sense of possibility, there is no energy to build. There is a sense of ending, of death. Not long ago, I lectured in Bloemfontein,

41

in the Orange Free State of the Republic of South Africa, where within five years a community of 300 families has become one of 195. It is clear that five years from now, there will not be 100. A few have gone to the State of Israel, a few to this country, and many to Johannesburg and Cape-Town. There, too, the evidence is plain—and depressing.

Nor is the decline of populations restricted to the smaller communities. We have to take into account as well the demographic facts facing American Jewry at large, the State of Israel's loss of one out of every ten of its population to other countries (over 300,000 out of 3 million Israelis live outside the State) and equivalent figures for assimilation, marriage out of Jewry, a low birth rate, and similar, disheartening phenomena all over the Jewish world.

But the real problem, of course, is not so much numbers, and everyone knows it. Numbers hide something more difficult to face. The Jews can go forward as a group, and Judaism as a religion, even if we are not so numerous as we currently are. So long as a demographic point of no return has not been crossed, the community may endure. The thing that troubles is the absence, within Jewry, of sizable numbers of people who derive any personal joy and meaning from being Jewish. There is a sad routineness to being Jewish, a passivity and dependence upon others. These traits, more than declining numbers, are deeply disturbing, for they mean that Judaism will soon lose the vitality it still enjoys, that larger numbers of Jews will lose even the tenuous relationship they currently maintain.

To be very blunt: in this country, most Jews get little personal satisfaction either out of being Jewish or out of Judaism. Most Jews pay their Jewish dues, both social and psychological, and their philanthropic taxes as well. But if you ask people, "What is it about being Jewish that you genuinely enjoy?," the answers are not encouraging. When you ask graduating college students, "What is your best and your worst Jewish experience?," many report that they have never had a "best" or a really "good" Jewish experience. And all name "Hebrew school" as their worst.

Where is Judaism to find the inner strength, the substance rooted in the lives of people, for the coming generations? I frankly do not know, because the Jews I see find little to sustain their Jewish daily lives; they do not live Jewish daily lives. But if being Jewish is not an everyday thing, then being Jewish no longer is a way of living. And if that is the case—if Judaism is deprived of its centrality as a way of life, so that the simplest Jewish rites are totally alien—then what is left? I do not mean what is left for the living. I mean what is left for those to come?

If, therefore, we look at the Jewish world around us, it is difficult not to engage in that classic and characteristic exercise of seeing ourselves as disappearing. And perhaps to feel that our generation is more genuinely entitled to the premonition of death than any that came before. Indeed, none of the propositions I have laid out is particularly startling. Some I first spoke of as long as twenty years ago. So Rawidowicz was correct in describing our generation. As much as any prior generation in all of Jewish history, more, perhaps, than most, we believe about ourselves that "with us the great tradition ends." We believe it in our small communities and in our large, in Africa, in Europe and in Latin America, in Australia, here in the United States, and, in some ways, even in the State of Israel.

No. No, no, not only because it ought not be, because it is not. Our "ever-dying" community is also a living community, and before we wrap ourselves in a smothering shroud, there are fundamental criticisms of the melancholy perspective that need to be heard. Hearing them, we learn that the luxury of melancholy and the habit of self-pity do not withstand examination.

For while it is true that there will likely be no Jewish community at all in Bloemfontein in the year 2000, and none in Kimberly by 1990, and perhaps none in a half-dozen or so American cities where communities now exist, that obviously does not mean that there will be no communities anywhere. We have lived in many places, and none is holier than the next. Kimberly in its day, Providence in its day, Afula in its day, no less, no more than the great centers of our past; each comes to

the fore, each passes on. What matters is not that there are
Jews in this place or in that, but that there are Jews. And what
matters still more is that there be Jews of quality and of
character. What matters is not whether there is, or will one day
be, a final resting place. What matters is that in the meanwhile,
the people endures, wherever it may be.

Do we endure? For all the talk of death, there are important
signs of life to notice.

Let me return to Rawidowicz, for he stated this point very
well:

"One often gets the impression that many . . . of the spiritual
leaders and spokesmen of traditional Israel in the last centuries
saw before them the imminent disappearance of the Sabbath,
the end of tefillin, piety, *yirat shamayim* (fear of heaven) and
faith in general. These centuries are today considered by us as
a kind of flowering of Jewish thought and life. Those great
Jews, whom we regard as important inaugurators of Jewish
values and ideas . . . saw themselves as the last guardians of a
treasure that would soon disappear forever."

There was a leading poet of the Haskalah, who wrote (cited
also by Rawidowicz), "For whom do I labor? Who will tell me
the future, will tell me that I am not the last poet of Zion, and
you my last readers?" But during the very time of Y. L.
Gordon, who wrote these lines, Haim Nahman Bialik was
growing up. So Gordon despaired, when Bialik, also Tchernichovsky, and yet others were coming to the fore. He despaired,
because he could not see. It is a sin for a Jew to despair. Bialik
for his part also saw himself as the end of the end, and a
convention in the Hebrew writing of the first half of this
century—the century which saw the creation of the State of
Israel and the renaissance of the Hebrew language—is that
these are the last Jewish writers, writing for the last Jews.

Now when we contemplate the American Jewish community, we follow this same convention, this ritualistic melancholy. We count too few; we are not happy with the caliber of
leadership; we find nothing but decay. Is there not something
to place on the other side of the balance?

I think there is a great deal, though we shall not appreciate our accomplishments and gain strength from them if we wish to luxuriate in self-pity. For one thing, American Jews have shaped that mode of Jewishness which is found useful throughout the Jewish world of the Golah. It has its faults, but it is surely not a negligible achievement that we have found a way. For another, there is, at this very time, an extraordinary renaissance of Jewish intellectual life, Jewish thought, Jewish scholarship, Jewish learning, and Jewish teaching, and it is happening in America and Canada. Today, apart from a few European-trained scholars who survive, the State of Israel is second in Jewish scholarship of the creative kind to American Jewry, in most, though not all, of the fields of Jewish learning. When you consider that learning to us is the object of labor, that we are not raised in Jewish texts and in the Hebrew language, you realize that even for us to be competitive with the Israelis is an achievement. But we turn out to be more than competitive, as proved by the numerous appointments of American Jews, and American-trained Jews, in the fields of Jewish learning in Israeli universities.

Yet another achievement of American Jewry is its present political alertness. Things we could not do thirty years ago we can do today. American Jews have achieved a capacity to make their wishes known and to persuade the larger political community to take these wishes seriously. This is an achievement. It did not come from Heaven. It was something people did for themselves.

These are the achievements of the elite, of the people in scholarship and in Jewish studies, in political life, in business. What shall we say of us all?

Here I think we have to point to an achievement so obvious that we cannot reckon with its worth: we have learned how to form and transmit some form of a Jewish pattern of life in this country. Obviously, none of us is satisfied with that pattern, nor can we even be proud of it. But when you consider that the fathers and mothers and the grandparents of the present generation were entirely unable to transmit their mode of being

Jewish to their children, you realize what has been accomplished. That is, the immigrant generation was a success in the shaping of a generation at home in America, and that was the immigrant generation's highest aspiration, and naturally so. But the immigrant generation transmitted nothing, beyond personal example, of a Jewish way of life. And a Jewish way of life reduced to aspects of ethnic culture is hopeless.

The immigrants, to name one thing, used Yiddish, but their children did not. So Yiddish died out. They may have come from a very strict way of life, but their children rarely took up that way of life. What the children got from the parents, by way of a Jewish way of life, was a folk culture of rather unimpressive character.

Now when you consider the demands that being Jewish makes upon us, the demands to be different from the majority, to marry other Jews, to eat different food and live a different sort of life, you must wonder whether it is worth doing all these things just to participate in a folk culture which cannot yield decent cooking. Why be Jewish in order to get a belly ache? Who needs it? The point is that the way of being Jewish which we know today is our own way; it was not bequeathed to us by the immigrant generation.

It was in part the second, and in part the third generation of American Jews which found their way to a mode of Judaism and an expression of Jewishness such as we now know. I do not mean to praise it, but I also do not think it is time to bury it. One thing is clear: that this mode of Judaism and this expression of Jewishness are something we can transmit to our children. And our forefathers and mothers did not create a mode of Judaism and an expression of Jewishness which they could transmit to their children. This generally accepted pattern, for all its faults, is something which has endured in America and does endure today. I wonder how many people realize that, two or three generations ago, most people were fairly sure there would be no Jews in America by the end of the twentieth century. And we now may be reasonably certain that there will be Jews in America at that time and for some time thereafter.

If it is true that we are not dying, and I do not think we are, even though, in this place or in that, there will be drastic changes, then what is happening to us? Why is it that we witness this dread, this foreboding, this sense of impending doom? It is an important question, because so long as our thoughts are melancholy, we shall be paralyzed and find ourselves too tired to do the work of the day. What we fear will happen we shall make happen.

Why is it that we see ourselves as a dying people, we who look back upon the longest continuous history among all the peoples of the world? Rawidowicz has this to say:

"I am often tempted to think that this fear of cessation in Israel was fundamentally a kind of protective individual and collective emotion. Israel has indulged so much in the fear of its end, that its constant vision of the end helped it to overcome every crisis, to emerge from every threatening end as a living unit, though much wounded and reduced. In anticipating the end, it became its master. Thus no catastrophe could ever take this endfearing people by surprise, so as to put it off its balance, still less to obliterate it—as if Israel's incessant preparation for the end made this very end absolutely impossible."

This is yet another insight we owe to Professor Rawidowicz, that the self-understanding of the Jewish people is part of its protection. For if we fear we are dying, we take those protective measures which will secure our future.

That may be natural, but I think there is a price to be paid, and it should be specified. It is not wise to dwell too much upon the future, as though it were more than what, in substantial measure, we make of it. If we become persuaded that we are doomed, we shall cease those healthy efforts at self-criticism and those successful efforts at self-improvement which already have made so much difference. The luxurious melancholy will paralyze us and make us think we have a power over the future independent of what we do in the present. What we have to learn from our fears for our own future is to look deeply into an unsatisfactory, but not hopeless, present.

Rawidowicz says, "A nation dying for thousands of years means a living nation. Our incessant dying means uninter-

rupted living, rising, standing up, beginning anew." If we may
go back to the premonitions of Jewish dissolution of the 1920's,
we gain hope and not discouragement at the achievements
even of the 1930's and 1940's. If we remember the fears of the
19th-century rabbis and scholars, we shall be pleasantly sur-
prised at the disproof of those fears.

We have to regard everything Jewish and enduring as remarkable. Then we shall appreciate what we have and so
understand how much better we can be. Perhaps to be sur-
prised by what we have, we have to fear for the future, so that
we may deem remarkable and amazing the small attainments
of the hour. But that is the only value I can see in the obsession
with "the end of the Jewish people" and with annihilation from
within.

From the moment of birth we are destined to death. But
what a glorious interval, what a splendid in-between! The
Jewish people too is dying. But it has taken a long time and will
take a long time to do it. And it seems to me that while there
will be changes, even changes we may not understand or
approve, still, in the end, we shall be very long in dying,
whatever happens in this place or that place, however much it
means to us in particular, where we happen to be at some one
moment. We have to learn how to die, so that, in the interval,
we may do a good job of living.

Part Two

Golah and Shoah

6. Beyond Catastrophe, Before Redemption

The issues of the murder of most of the Jews in continental Europe between 1933 and 1945 not only are obscured, but also are rendered abstract and remote, by the language we have adopted to discuss those issues. The word "Holocaust," of course, is the principal offender, with "Auschwitz," with or without its "after," running a close second. This language treats as one and single a myriad of awful events. It serves, indeed, to reduce to an abstract symbol of language those concrete events of death and destruction which, one by one, make of the murder of the Jews of Europe an awesome and truly ineffable tragedy. I think that, in this way, we have carried forward that creation of a dehumanizing language about which George Steiner wrote, the formation of a kind of German vocabulary which both refers to concrete action and denies that action any sort of reality and specificity: "special handling" to refer to murder, "resettlement" to refer to shipment of human beings in cattle cars to gas chambers, and other euphemisms.

"Holocaust," after all, before the recent past, was not used to refer to things people do to people, but to the way in which priests offer up cows and bulls. "Extermination" is what is done to insects. "Auschwitz" is not really allowed to be one place among many; it is forced to stand for the homogenization of all places into one, all experiences into a single experience of

51

death, all personal tragedies (and they are beyond counting) into a single thing: encapsulated in a word, reduced to a word, controlled by a word. If some people have responded in a bitter way and referred to the public-relations circus which has enveloped the murder of the Jews of Europe as "Shoah, Incorporated," or said, "There is no business like Shoah-business," they can be forgiven their bitterness. They speak a truth about exploitation. Let the truth be told.

Now, in point of fact, what we have done is to make the murder of the Jews of Europe into one of the principal components of the civil religion of American Jews. That is the religion expressed on neutral, non-religious occasions, to make sense of and celebrate our community, its distinctiveness, its program, its demands upon ourselves. Why is this possible? The reason that that murder serves so well is that it is only part of a complete account. The murder of the European Jews, turned into a symbol and made into a mythic account of who we are, poses a question. And the question is answered by the other half of that component of our civil religion, the half which speaks of redemption. That half posits a redemption brought about through the creation of the State of Israel. So the whole Torah of our day is the story, effectively captured by the Israeli version of the same civil religion, of *shoah u'gevurah*, Holocaust and heroism.

Now in the Israeli context, this civil religion is apt and fitting, since it not only speaks of the past, but it explains the present. The story of *shoah u'gevurah* explains who an Israeli is, why Israelis must do the things they do, and what the forces of Jewish destiny have done to make them what they are. For the State of Israel confronts persistent insecurity and danger. But Israelis in their state also exercise that heroism to survive the perpetual confrontation. That is the theory of who they are, and it explains, too, the fittingness, the adequacy, of what we may call, "the myth of Holocaust and redemption," that is, the story, abidingly true, always relevant to here and now of the Jewish State, the story of death and resurrection, annihilation and rebirth, the account of the individual and the people passing through hell to something very like a fulfilled and redeemed age, the passage from death to rebirth.

It is a perfectly natural effort to explain people to themselves, in terms of experience they have had and now have, in terms of a world of perennial danger but also of opportunity to confront and overcome danger. The myth of Holocaust and redemption, in its form of *shoah u'gevurah*, is profoundly well suited to the existential facts of the State of Israel.

What that myth does in *our* context, however, is not so obvious. Indeed, it seems to me curiously inappropriate.

First of all, when we address the realities of the murder of European Jews in their millions, we must recognize that our realities, our sense of ourselves and our circumstances, are not so different from those in which they lived and died. Now, whether or not America is different is not really at issue. The point is that by harping on the murder of the European Jews we create in ourselves a fearful sense of dread and dislocation. We express that perfectly natural fear that it can happen again, that the world has not much changed, and that we live amid danger as much as did the Jews of Poland, Czechoslovakia, or France, in the time of German hegemony. This part of the matter, this expression of the fear of neighbor which is real, gains strength in what I think for many of us is a recurrent nightmare, in which we die in gas chambers or on the streets. Indeed, if the truth must be told, I wonder whether there are many Jews in America who can pass an entire week without for one moment reflecting on what might be and what might have been. I doubt there are many who do not have that concentration-camp nightmare which wakes me up more than seldom. It is the given of our life.

But the reason is not what happened then. It is what we fear may happen now. The power and truth of myth is there: in its capacity to capture and explain today, in its acute relevance to this hour. So in a time in which American Jews enjoy unprecedented status in public life, unimagined freedom of access to all careers and institutions to which they might aspire, American Jews also find themselves ridden with fears for their lives and their future. That is what, I think, this constant allusion to places with strange names in distant parts of the world, means about us. We speak of ourselves. We talk of the here and now. But we have found for ourselves a private and distinctive language to capture and express our fears and our sense of self.

Clearly, there is truth in our fears. But there also can be excessive fear, a preoccupation with what might be, yielding paralysis before good things which now are. No one knows what will be. All we can control—if that—is what we are, what we wish to become. And to this exercise in constructing a viable future for ourselves in Judaism, in America, the murder of the Jews of Europe has its contribution to make, but only in a measure. It is to be placed in the vast context of the history of the Jewish people and interpreted in the profound and richly tragic perspective of Judaism as a way of understanding the world and interpreting who we are. The Shoah is a part of a mode of framing a way of life congruent to our understanding of the world and relevant to who we are. Placed in that framework of Judaism, the murder of the Jews of Europe constitutes one of the chapters of deepest insight, most pro-found meaning. It is one of the truest messages in the history of the Jewish people and in the history of Judaism. But it can be received only within that whole, complete context of Judaism and of the history of the Jewish people, a Judaism of suffering but also of celebration, joy, and worth. Treated as a moment which dictates the meaning of the whole, this moment of mass murder distorts the whole.

For we cannot live our lives and raise our children to live their lives in total distrust of our circumstance, in complete denial of our own power, too, to shape our destiny and change the world in which we live. The Holocaustomania has given us just as unreal a view of the world in which we live as would an effort completely to obliterate the memory of the murder of the European Jewry by their fellow-citizens in many countries. Such a criminal act of ignoring would give us an unreal view of the world in which we live. The potentiality for Jew-hatred is ever present. So is the fact. But the Jews are also not without power in their various countries. Still more important, the murderers of European Jewry cannot be taken to be ubiquitous. We do not live among murderers. We ourselves are not victims of murderers. The turning of the murder of European Jewry into a paramount symbol of what it means to be a Jew presents altogether too simple and too repulsive an account of reality.

In point of fact, the tasks before us are to build a Jewish community among people who have decided they wish to be Jews, to bear the risks of being Jews in America. What is needed is a theory of ourselves, an explanation of what we think our being Jewish requires of us and means to us. I do not mean the work is to explain why we should be Jewish. That is a decision we have already made. It is now, how should we be Jewish? Now, in my view, the need for a clear explanation of the wide range of choices before us (I regard them all as legitimate and equally honest) is paramount. One response to this question is forthcoming from the theologians of catastrophe who have placed "after Auschwitz" at the center of their discourse and treated the perennial problem of evil as probative and definitive of the Jewish and human condition. That response tells us we must be Jewish "because we should not hand Hitler any more victories." But the logical problem we then confront is: how should we be Jewish under the aspect of Nazism? What are the things we do because we do not wish to hand Hitler any more victories? I ask these questions on the assumption that they are irrelevant, because there is no reasonable and pertinent answer, no answer we can use in the formation of our homes and our families. The Holocaust-theologians do not ask the question we must answer.

The reason that the use of the murders of European Jews in the formation of a theory of American Judaism is hopeless now must be specified. It is because, without some form of redemption, such as the Israelis supply for themselves, "the Holocaust" is not a component in a viable myth. We cannot shape our lives around such awful events alone. We cannot raise our children to understand that being Jewish leads them through such terrible experience alone. Without a story of redemption, a story about ourselves and our circumstances we can feel and believe, the story of death, annihilation, destruction, the murder of millions of people, the obliteration of ancient civilization, the end of our old, enduring cities gives us nothing to build on. What is the point of dwelling on suffering, without consolation, on death without rebirth? I see none.

Now, we tell ourselves that the consolation is the creation of the State of Israel, and that is true. The rebirth of the Jewish people takes place through the achievement of the Zionist movement, and that is true. But it is true for someone else. It is not true for ourselves. We are not there. We are here. When we tell ourselves there is a resurrection, it is not of our body, not of ourselves. So we speak of someone else's death in Europe and someone else's rebirth in the Land. The myth is serviceable, but not for a world in which *we* live, I mean, we who did not suffer personally in the European catastrophe, and also did not participate, and do not participate, personally, in the Israeli defiance of catastrophe.

Ours is a mythic situation in which we talk about what other people go through, but then we find ourselves unable to explain the world in which we live, the things through which we pass, the life which we choose for ourselves and our children. We are spectators at someone else's drama. But life is not for spectators. We pretend to be what we are not, not victims or survivors, not builders or Israelis. We know full well that we do not want to be what we never were, and what even now we do not choose to be: we are not survivors, who were born and brought up in this country, and we are not those who in the Land defy and overcome. We choose without apology or guilt to make our lives right here, right now.

That is why, as I said, we cannot work out that theory of ourselves, of who we are and what we are, that story of what we dream of being and of how we shall surpass ourselves and overcome the obstacles of our being—we cannot work out that theory of ourselves, because the materials with which we try to work are unworkable, intractable. Nearly everything we do as

Jews, apart from the personal practice of the Jewish religion, bears no relationship to nearly everything we are. It is as simple, in my view, as that: most of what we do in our life-situation as Jews simply bears no close relevance to what we are as frail, suffering, wondering women and men.

I am worried about the health of my close colleague. I am concerned about the illness of the son of my best friend. I am eager to see my own children grow into worthwhile adults. I want to be a good husband to my wife. I am trying to make sense of my work as a teacher, of my use to my students. I would like to find something of more than casual or episodic meaning in my week-to-week encounter with my own being as a Jew, I mean, in the *minyan* which I cherish. That is my short list. I can make a much longer list.

And I offer it as an example only, in order to stimulate other people to make their lists of their problems, the things which they have to work out. Where my heart is—there must be the story of who I am. Now to these lists, what is the relevance, what the significance, what the probative value, of the murders of European Jews or the expulsion from Spain, for that matter? Why should there be something called a "Holocaust center"? What does it say, which I do not hear from Job? What is there to see, which I do not see in the suffering of my friend's son? As I said, the Israelis understand so much more deeply what is demanded, for theirs are centers of *shoah u'gevurah*, "Holocaust and heroism." Our public Jewish life thus is irrelevant to our private, human life; theirs is deeply relevant.

We who move toward what, I suppose, we may call a post-modern world do not move a single step beyond that position in which, forever and for all time, we have been standing—we who have a mountain hanging over our heads.

7. After the Flood; After the Rainbow

Last month, "Holocaust." This month, Israel Independence Day. A coupling in time that reflects with uncanny accuracy the contemporary Jewish understanding, an understanding that has come to inform virtually every aspect of our communal life—that Jewish life is the story of Holocaust-to-Redemption.

What does it mean to be an American Jew these days? For many people, the definition is remarkably straightforward: it means to accept the Holocaust-to-Redemption myth as central to one's theology, even to one's psychology. It means to be seized by the death-and-resurrection metaphor, and to view the world through its lenses.

It could scarcely be otherwise. In all of Jewish time, there are not a dozen dates that will be remembered so long as there are Jews to remember things, and two of those dates occurred within our own living memory. It is entirely natural that our lives have been shaped by the events which those dates mark.

And it is entirely understandable that in the shaping, there has been distortion. We can hardly expect that those still in the thrall of the events will manage the perspective that only distance permits. But that does not free us from the need to ask not only what it means to be a Jew in contemporary America, but also what it *might* mean, what it *should* mean.

Ours is the fourth generation. It is different from what we have known until now. Assimilation is no longer an interesting

58

or an attractive ideology. By and large, those who wanted out of Jewish life are gone. At the same time, oddly, marriage to non-Jews has become an open (and increasingly popular) choice for those who have stayed, who have stayed Jews. Nor is that choice any longer attended by the guilt and recrimination which it invariably invoked a short time ago. More often than not, the non-Jew is received into the Jewish family with relative ease.

These apparently contradictory trends describe the world of the fourth generation: unashamedly Jewish, unselfconsciously American, open to whatever the world has to say, but still unclear about what to listen for or even how to hear.

How is it that we have come to receive the non-Jew into our midst with such ease? It is because to join the Jewish group is to join a world not very different from the world the non-Jew has left. Indeed, the differences between ourselves and our non-Jewish neighbors have become so trivial that we do a better job, on the whole, of assimilating non-Jews into our midst than of assimilating Russian and Israeli Jews. And that, plainly, is because being Jewish is not nearly so distinctive as once it was. It hardly involves profound changes of outlook or behavior; mostly, it implies a shift in cultural and social ambience. The shift, on the whole, is to a higher social, economic, and cultural status; to marry a Jew is to marry up. And to marry a non-Jew is to bring to the Jewish fold people whose knowledge, background and commitment are not much different from the prevailing norms of the Jewish community, sometimes even to provide fresh energies for the community.

So here we are, in a time of renewed enthusiasm, profound and completed acculturation, substantial non-ideological assimilation, and genuine social integration—a mass of contradictions that provide the context for the next decade of American Jewish life.

It comes as something of a surprise, of course. When, in the crucible of Vietnam, American young people turned against that white, Protestant, middle class conventional conception of our society which had in their eyes proved its moral bankruptcy, substantial numbers turned instead to their own ethnic roots—with the blacks leading the way. In the light of the third generation Jewish consensus, one might have predicted that Jews would follow this trend lamely if at all. For the third generation, which flourished from the end of World War II to the end of the Vietnam War, had adopted as its working slogan, "Be Jewish—but not too Jewish." Why "Be Jewish?" Because anti-Semitism was still a problem; to cease to be Jewish would have been dishonorable. Why "not too Jewish?" because that would mean barring access to the American dream. The promised land cannot be entered by those with foreign accents.

But the children of the third generation could not fail to see the contradiction. Some resolved it by not being Jewish at all, a more attractive option during a time when anti-Semitism did not appear to be a clear or present danger. Others chose instead to be massively and militantly Jewish. Whatever the blacks could do, they could do better.

But like the Russian Jews who want to be Jewish, their motive has outstripped their competence. The best they have been able to do is to experiment with the forms of "being Jewish," an experiment which is often religious in its style and empty in its substance. Blacks want soul food? Then we shall have kosher food, and if that proves too difficult, then at least bagels on Sunday. The issue for this generation of good intention was not Judaism but instead, the visible symbols and signs of "being Jewish." And the striking modes of Jewishness they have adopted show clearly the results of the assimilation that has gone before.

Thus: one sign of "being Jewish" which many of the young have adopted is the wearing of a *kippah* under all circumstances. Normally, when we see a *kippah*, we feel entitled to assume many other forms of observance—at least, one would suppose, eating kosher food and observing all aspects of the Sabbath. What, then, are we to make when we see a *kippah*-ed head bent over a hamburger at the local McDonalds? Or what of a group of American kids wearing *kippot* riding the bus in Tel Aviv on Shabbat?

The adoption of superficial religious symbols is only one form, and not the most popular, for the new Jewish self-expression. Instead, the majority of newly revived Jews—of whatever age—have adopted as their central path of access to Judaism the Holocaust-to-Redemption myth. This tale, with its obvious moral, is drummed into our heads by every medium of Jewish communication. It has become our fixation, the source of our metaphor as of our self-understanding, the primary energizer of Jewish life and the primary axiom of Jewish logic.

How did the Holocaust become so powerful a symbol? Before 1967, it was not. A whole generation had refused to pay attention, to be reminded, to confront. How is it that so suddenly there is a genuine popular response to Jewish theologians who create what they call "Holocaust theologies" and who hold solemn meetings in cathedrals on "Judaism after Auschwitz" and the like?

The answer lies in the 1967 War and in the weeks that preceded it. During those weeks, we feared the worst. Unlike others whose fears are born of fantasy, ours are born of memory. We have a name for our worst fears, and the name we have is Auschwitz. In those weeks of May and June, we foresaw the end of the Jewish State, and even—some thought—the end of the Jewish People. We trembled, and we knew, out of our own experience, the fear of destruction. We knew the sense of Auschwitz.

And then, even as we were feeling terror, we knew triumph. The Holocaust was not merely averted; it was over, it would no longer be the central theme of Jewish life. We had entered the post-Holocaust era. And what is that era save the time of salvation, of the Messiah? When we returned to the Wall, Jewish history as we had known it came to an end.

The fact that the 1967 War created as many problems as it solved, that the triumph of arms led to a spirit of imperial triumphalism for which, in the end, both the State of Israel and the Jewish People are still paying the price—these facts were seen only by a few.

Then the Holocaust theologians, journalists, publicists, fund raisers, organizers, speakers, novelists—the whole phalanx of

Jewish public relations—took up the theme of salvation through politics, the fantastic and hopeless pronouncement of beginning of redemption. A messianic fervor swept over the Jewish people, both there and here, and on that fervor were built the flawed structures of consciousness and culture which today we see about us. Anyone who could cite a few passages from Scripture and put on a good cry in public became a Judaic theologian, and the more tears, the more profound he seemed to be.

It is a mark of the assimilation expressed through ethnic assertion that the old Jewish reservation about messianism is scarcely remembered. For to understand our people's long history of nay-saying in the face of false messiahs, both Jewish and gentile, we have to know our people's equally long history of yea-saying to Torah and its claim to sanctify the present and to regain in the here-and-now a foretaste of eternity.

Holocaust-and-Redemption-theology is easy and appeals to people with no access to Jewish piety, learning, tradition. Further, the powerful appeal well serves the interests of people who know precisely what they want from our community—the fund raisers.

So they organize their ghoulish trips to Auschwitz and to Jerusalem, make the memory of dead people into an instrument for the guilt and coercion of the living, and represent Judaism as a religion for cemeteries and battlefields. Judaism, a religion of the present and the future, affirms life and looks not to Auschwitz but to Sinai. But the Judaism of Sinai has not been heard from much these days, and the life-giving symbols and signs of Torah have been obscured by clouds of death and hot air. Hitler is represented as a negative symbol, rather than Moses as a positive one. So we are told we should be Jewish not because God has called us into being but in order to spite Hitler.

A more spurious argument has never been put forth onto the stage of Judaic thought, a more ignorant and a more destructive conception of the wellsprings of Judaism has never been drawn before our people's eyes. But many were served, ignoramuses pretending to be learned, fund raisers seeking easy access to emotions, but, too, people of good intention who had no clear notion of what they had to do to achieve their good intention: to be Jewish again.

There is, yet, the other half of the Holocaust-and-Redemption theory of Jewish existence, the Redemption part. This, of course, has been expressed in the notion that the State of Israel has solved the Jewish problem, has given us reason to be Jewish and therefore serves as the center and the focus of Jewish consciousness. Once more it is obvious that that idea has well served the practical administrators of Jewry. But it also has spoken to, and for, the Jewish masses, among whom I include myself. For to a very real measure our Jewish lives respond first and foremost to what is happening in Jerusalem, and Judaism, as well as contemporary Jewish politics, surely teaches that that is an authentic and healthy Jewish emotion.

Yet it also is the best evidence for my thesis that we are both ethnically assertive and profoundly assimilated. When we get past the fund raising (and, it is clear, no successful Jewish fund raising in America and Canada is possible without a massive Israeli component), we must ask: to what extent does the State of Israel, its religion, culture, intellectual life, shape, or even contributing to the shaping of, American and Canadian Jewish life?

I find the answer ambiguous. On the one side all of us come to life when the State of Israel is in crisis. The response to the 1967 and 1973 Wars is very profound. The emotional commitment of the community surely was tested and found authentic and real. On the other hand, when we transcend the emotional concern and begin to ask about cultural and intellectual aspects of American Jewish affairs, the picture is very different.

Thus: to what extent does American Jewry make use of modern Hebrew? We have now sent tens of thousands of young people to study in Israel for summers or for whole school years. If Hebrew were going to be a significant factor in our community, the opportunity is here. Yet with all the investment of young peoples' lives in study of Hebrew both here and there, we may say that Hebrew is not part of American Jewish culture.

To what extent is American Jewry involved in the inner life of the Israeli Jewish world? Do we read its books and talk about them? Apart from a few novels in English we certainly do not. Do we follow the everyday events of their politics and institutions? Only in the public press, along with other Americans.

Do we gain access to Jewish classics through Israeli scholarship? Apart from a few scholars of European origin and a handful of archaeologists and other biblical specialists, Israeli scholarship makes virtually no impact whatsoever upon American Jewish intellectual life. It makes slight enough impact even upon the American Jewish scholars who read Hebrew and can mediate the results of Israeli scholarship to the American Jewish public.

In the vast growth of Jewish studies in American universities, the study of Israeli society and culture (when we omit reference to a semester of conversational Hebrew) is minimal. The students are not interested. Neither are their parents. Israeli studies do not form a considerable part of what we understand as Jewish studies, because, I suspect, they do not answer questions we propose to ask when we undertake Jewish studies.

We need not mince words. Apart from our deep concern for the welfare of the State of Israel and its people, we really are not much interested in the State of Israel or in Zionism. We are all aware of how much the Arabs have done to make Zionism an important issue for the Jewish people, and for that we are grateful. But it is difficult to discern a renaissance of Zionist theory, a reconsideration of classical and perennial issues of Zionist thought, in the current renewal of Zionist loyalty.

So if we American Jews are Zionists, that does not mean we want to say more than that we are Zionists. We do not for one minute propose to shape our thinking about ourselves in response to the issues of Zionist theory, past or present.

My thesis is clear. American Jews over the past decade have entered a period of Jewish assertion, but have yet to make up their minds about what it is that they propose to assert. And what they do assert turns out, on close examination, to be a superficial and assimilated thing, even while it looks on the surface to be the most Jewish thing of all. Holocaust-and-Redemption theories of Jewish assertion, chugging along with all the power of the mighty engines of Jewish organization life, on the one side, and fed by the fuel of those deep Jewish emotions to which they appeal, on the other, lead nowhere. The reason is that their basic goal and direction do not relate to the realities in which American Jews live out their lives.

Holocaust-Redemption theories speak of a world of historical events, of upheaval, a world destroyed and recreated, a human experience of degradation and restoration. But American Jews of the third and fourth generations know about such experiences only in books. They can be asked to pretend they were there, they can make pilgrimages and shiver in Auschwitz, or dance at the Wall. But these are vicarious emotions. We are confronted with a theory of Jewish existence which speaks of the world we do not know, and which carefully ignores the world we do inhabit.

We have lived in a peaceful, progressive, and reasonably prosperous country. The Jews in this country are not weak and persecuted. They are not in need of a refuge. They do not even know the meaning of anti-Semitism in its political sense, and their knowledge of racism is gained in newspapers. True, they do know discrimination and have experienced social and cultural anti-Semitism of various kinds, even the religious sort.

But the anti-Semitism which led inexorably to Auschwitz—and therefore, also to Jerusalem—is not part of our experience, and theories of Jewish existence which explain a world of metahistorical evil and eschatological redemption simply do not refer to our humble reality at all.

That is why our theories of what it means to be a Jew in contemporary America all emerge as flawed. They talk about experiences we have not had, except in our nightmares, and ask us to accept a redemption which does not save us from anything from which we need to be saved, nor promise us a salvation which solves the real problems we must confront.

First, whatever theory of Jewish existence we propose to

shape must be relevant to our situation as human beings, as Jews, as a distinctive group of human beings who choose to be Jews. The particular point of relevance, moreover, must be to those profound human problems which all of us must solve, and which we have to confront together, if our being Jews is to matter at the deepest levels of our lives. For let us face honestly and squarely that very difficult fact, which we pretend to ignore: we are deeply assimilated to this country and its life. Just as grotesque as are the Russian refuseniks, who dance in the streets on Simchat Torah, because they know it is a holiday, but are not quite sure what to make of it, so grotesque are we in our ways.

And yet, assimilated as we are, we do choose to be Jews, and to assert our Jewishness and give shape to our lives through Judaism. That too is a difficult fact, which we of course take for granted: as deeply as we are part of the common life, so profoundly do we exhibit signs of being a distinctive group. These then are the parameters of theory. I do not know how we shall fill those outlines with color and meaning. I do know that theories of Jewish existence which ignore who and where and what we are will never serve us for very long.

Second, however we propose to explore the meaning of our Jewishness and ask what it means to be a Jew here and now, the exploration—the hard work of learning and discovery—must be done by all of us, not only by a few on behalf of many. Our character as highly educated men and women, our careers at the upper levels of society and politics and economy and industry and education, our commitment to freedom and free thought, our acknowledgement of our independence and our respect for our own judgments—these traits cannot be ignored when we undertake the quest, in the sources of Judaism and of Jewish culture, for a usable past and a credible future.

If there is anything pernicious in the Holocaust-and-Redemption theory of Jewish existence, it is that it leaves the ordinary folk with no worthwhile tasks, no meaningful assignments. No theory of Jewish existence will speak to us which says only, "Give and be saved. Cry and feel saved. Make a trip to Israel and be forever saved." No theory of Jewish existence will persuade us of its sense which says only, "Listen and do what you're told." Nor will American Jews continue to concede that the true and authentic Jewish life is possible only elsewhere. For if they do agree and yet stay just where they are, then their Jewishness will atrophy and die.

Before us all is the task of framing a vision and a hope, of shaping a purpose and a dream, worthy of our situation as Jews, relevant to our lives, appropriate to our condition as free and self-reliant men and women, and above all authentic to our calling as part of the Jewish people, the Israel which forms the center of human history and destiny.

8. Other Times, Other Places, Us

To what question is "the Holocaust and the Redemption" the answer?

That it is an answer is plain. For these events, far from America's shores and remote from the everyday experience of America's Jews, constitute the central myth by which American Jews seek to make sense of themselves and to decide what to do with that (sizable) part of themselves which is set aside for "being Jewish." Are we not bound to ask how it is that people of the particular social and historical profile of the American Jews—fully acculturated Americans, with a considerable measure of educational and financial accomplishment—urgently construct for themselves a world in which they do not live, an ark they do not plan to stock and float? Why do they draw upon experiences they have not had and do not wish to have for their symbols and their myths, for their rites and their deeds?

To what question, then, are the stories of the destruction of European Jewry and the creation of the State of Israel, compelling—and to the believers, even self-evident—answers? What is it that American Jews want to know, feel they need to know, that draws them, moth-like, to the flames of other times and other places?

The puzzling thing is not that political events—the destruction of a group, the formation of a nation state—should inform the imagination of a people. Such large events generate social change and dislocation, and social change is the source of symbol change. Killing off the bulk of Europe's Jews involved a social change of profound and lasting consequence; setting up a Jewish state in the ancient homeland did as well. And these inevitably lead to symbol change, to a restructuring of the imagination.

No, what is puzzling is that such dislocation should be made into the permanent and normative condition of a group, that these remembered experiences should come to outweigh the experienced experiences of that group, that without the appropriation of these events the members of that group cannot make sense of themselves.

The shift in the symbolic life of those Jews fortunate enough to find their way to the Jewish state, the use of the destruction of European Jewry in the self-understanding of that state, the formation of a consequent symbolic structure which draws on the event and converts it into a myth and into a rite—all that is straightforward, plausible. Not so with America's Jews. That the same myth should be even more powerful, more fundamental here than it is there—that is the puzzle. Why it is that people choose to work out their sense of themselves and their society in terms essentially irrelevant to their ordinary world and everyday experience—that is the puzzle.

It is a puzzle I cannot solve. I live, as all who share the myth, on ground which is both not mine and not not-mine. The only lands which I know and the only languages which I use are, lands and languages both, the property of others. Why I should be a stranger there where I think I should be at home, whether in Jerusalem or Providence, I cannot say. I know only that there are norms, both there and here, both without and within, both social and deep within the heart, which insist *not* that I cannot go home again, but that I am not supposed to have a home, not now, not ever, not where I am, and not, in the nature of things, anywhere else. There is a persistent dissonance between where I am and who I want to be, and the myth of "Holocaust and Redemption" expresses that dissonance.

Who are these Jews who respond to the myth? They form the vast and vital center of American Jewry, with its wall-to-wall consensus on the importance of the State of Israel to the American Jews' own Judaism and on the self-evident truths yielded by the Holocaust. These are the Jews who do not wholly practice the disciplines of Judaism and also do not wholly neglect them. They take an active part in the life of the Jewish community, its synagogues, organizations, philanthropies, politics, and other practical activities, at the same time living a life essentially void of the spirituality and sensibility of Judaism. They know what the Holocaust means and they know what Redemption means; these twin notions are their Judaism, they lead to conclusions that have been reached in advance, they fix both world-view and way-of-life. And they have such status because they answer the basic questions of American Jewish life, questions that have to do with assimilation and with self-hatred.

The Holocaust—no, not the Holocaust, but "the Holocaust," not the event but the myth—captures our sense of dislocation and that fear of the rest of the world which is our lot. It expresses in an extreme way the potentialities of our pariah-status. Its message is stark and terrifying, too stark and too terrifying to serve, by itself, as an organizing myth. But when the myth is completed by the Redemption, "the Holocaust" becomes manageable, it takes on a different and acceptable dimension. "The Holocaust" asks the question which the Zionism that has been fulfilled by and in the State of Israel answers. The pariah-people triumphs over its worst catastrophe and creates its home in its ancient homeland.

For America's Jews, beset by the challenges of assimilation and overwhelmed by a sense of discomfort at their own (paltry) differences from the majority, the myth of Holocaust and Redemption serves both to express fear and to offer remission from it; it simultaneously explains the necessity of being Jewish and the possibility that others will bear the central burden of being Jewish. Our history has become our theology, our metaphysics. And it is our own circumstances, our own fears, our own perceptions that have accomplished the transformation. The extermination of European Jewry has been transformed into "the Holocaust" because we have needed it to be so transformed. Wanting intuitively, instinctively, to be Jewish, without knowing what that might mean, or, knowing, without being prepared to mean quite that, "the Holocaust" offers meaning and motive. It tells us why we must be Jewish, even in the absence of understanding. It justifies our confusion. And we are not terrified by it because the Redemption assures us that "the Holocaust" will not happen again, that all is not, in the end, absurd. Understanding is made possible by the Redemption; we are pointed in precise directions, there are tasks to be performed, there is meaning after all. We become Jewish "because" of "the Holocaust"; we act out our Jewishness by way of the Redemption—that is, by commitment to the State of Israel, that place which gives meaning and significance to and remission from the terror.

A theology, with rites and rituals. The rites of the redemptive myth involve attendance at ritual dinners at which money is given and at which Israel is celebrated, endless cycles of work in that same cause, rehearsal of the faith to outsiders and marginal Jews, trips to the State of Israel. The expressive modes which bring the motive and the myth alive revolve around celebration and support for the Jewish state.

In short: If you want to know why, and then how, to be Jewish, you have to remember that (1) the gentiles wiped out the Jews of Europe, and so are not to be trusted, let alone joined; (2) if there had been "Israel," meaning the State of Israel, there would have been no "Holocaust"; (3) it follows that for your own sake and for the sake of your children, in order to insure your personal safety and theirs, you have to "support Israel." You do not *have* to live there, but it is a mark of piety to feel guilty for not living there—a piety, like so many others, remarkably rare in American Jewish life.

This is the myth and these are the rituals, this is the answer we have fashioned. And the question? The question is: How shall we make sense out of our persistence in preserving a distinctive group life when we are thoroughly acculturated in America, when we are chronically (albeit not acutely) the victims of self-hatred, when we are at best marginally related to our own history, to the way of life and the world view of our ancestors, down to our grandparents?

American Judaism, then, is a wholly Zionist Judaism. Of course there are many American Jews to whom Zionism is simply unknown. But because the mythic importance of the State of Israel to American Judaism is so utterly fundamental, because the Zionist redemption is perceived as compensation and consolation for the death of six million European Jews, the Zionist perspective is the implicit heart of American Jewish life.

There can, however, be no discussion of Zionism within the American Jewish context without confronting the first and most direct judgment of Zionism upon world Jewry: All those Jews who do not live in Israel are in exile from Israel. The issue of *galut*, of exile, is the inescapable issue, and the contradiction between the Zionist faith of American Jewry and its self-willed exile is the inescapable contradiction. Around that contradiction all other discourse on Zionism must circle, weaving and bobbing, drawing near and moving far. In the end, all discourse is obsessed with that plain and painful contradiction.

What sort of Zionists are we, can we be, outside the State of Israel? What kind of Zionism is it that we pursue, or want to pursue, while having chosen for ourselves a permanent exile?

I cannot answer these questions. If I had worthy answers, I would offer them. I do not. I have no answers that satisfy.

I know that there are other questions which are no more tractable and which confront my counterparts across the oceans: What sort of Zionism do you contemplate that is different from the nationalism of the State of Israel? And if Zionism is principally identical with Israeli nationalism, then what do you have to say to the rest of the Jewish world, with its other nationalisms? And what do you have to say to the rest of your own population, which is not Jewish at all? But the beam in my eye will not be removed by my effort to magnify the mote in the eye of my fellow.

Simply stated, Zionism maintains that Jews who do not live in the Jewish state are in exile. There is no escape from the allegation; hence the facile affirmation of Zionism which is so central to American Judaism is necessarily called into question. For what manner of Zionism is it that can accommodate so massive and so voluntary an exile? Moreover, Zionism declares that Jews who do not live in the State of Israel must aspire to migrate there, or, at the least, to raise their children as potential immigrants. But American Jewry, Zionist though it be, chokes on that position. Finally, Zionism insists that Jews must not only concede, but actively affirm, the centrality of Jerusalem and of the State of Israel in the life of Jews throughout the world. Not merely the importance; the centrality. Implicitly—and sometimes explicitly—Zionism concludes that those Jews who live outside the State of Israel are in significant ways less "good Jews" than the ones who live there.

All these propositions are commonplace to Israeli Zionism. They are, further, passively accepted—at least in their benign verbal formulation—by American Jews. But they manifestly contradict the simple facts of the situation of American Jews and their Judaism.

American Jews do not think they are in exile. They may not feel fully at home, they may never; but not-home is not exile. The Judaism of American Jews makes no concession to the notion of exile.

Second, American Jews have not the remotest thought of emigrating from America to the State of Israel. It is true that on ceremonial occasions they will listen quietly as Israeli spokesmen declare such immigration to be their duty. But that is as far as it goes.

Third, American Jews ritually affirm the centrality of the State of Israel, and, at some level, accept the derivative inference—that is, the peripherality of the *Golah*, the Diaspora, including the mighty American Jewish community. It is precisely here that the Zionism of American Jews comes closest to telling the truth about American Jews—the truth that they do not take themselves or their future as Jews seriously. For were that not the case, the contradiction would be intolerable, and the myth would not be necessary.

The Zionist vision and its acceptance by American Jews tells us something very important about the self-image of those Jews. It tells us very little, however, about the commonplace realities of American Jews, no more, indeed, than "the Holocaust" tells us. So let us talk more about this matter of self-image, of self-understanding.

Let us talk again about exile. If there is to be a Zionism, there must be a Zion. And if there is a Zion, there is also a non-Zion; a Land without an outside-the-Land is not possible. Zion is not in Heaven; it is here on earth, in the material reality of the Land and the State of Israel. Exile, by the same token, is not merely an existential alienation; it is a concrete reality. Those who identify it with an aching heart—and Zion with the Messianic era—may have something to say to us, but that something is not about Zionism.

Zionism speaks of the flesh, of the this-worldly facts of Jewish political existence. And it speaks, therefore, of exile, of non-Zion, and it raises, therefore, the straightforward question: Are American Jews, are we, in exile? Or the tangential questions: Of what use is the notion of exile for us? What vision is it that we have of the world that so captures our attention as to make the Zionist perception persuasive to us?

We are a people who do this-worldly things, yet insist on wearing the prophet's cloak over our shoulders, the philosopher's mantle. We are a people who, with perfect confidence in our righteousness, seek salvation, pursue it. We are busy and we are practical, and we are also dreamers. We dream of salvation, and, in our time, what more compelling salvific dream is there than the dream of Zionism, Israel as the negation of meaninglessness, of chaos, of terror, of destruction, of the apocalypse.

But it must be added that Zionism is not, for most of us, a complete vision of salvation. Zionism promises redemption, but it does not offer sufficient redemption; it solves some problems, but not all the problems of the human condition, or even of the Jewish condition. (Indeed, the more we come to know about this-worldly Zionism, about the flesh-and-bone salvation it offers, the fewer problems it appears to resolve, the more it creates.)

Still, Zionism remains the single most powerful and most important movement in the history of the Jewish people in this century. The creation of the State of Israel is universally acknowledged to be the single most important achievement of the Jewish people in this time. It vastly overshadows the achievement of American Judaism. Above all, Zionism tells us, as does its creature, the State of Israel, that our fixation with salvation, with redemption, is not folly.

Hence there can be no evasion of the Zionist challenge to American Judaism, the Zionist defiance of American Jewry's comfortable and complacent situation. On the contrary, a Zionist theory of American Jewry—if a theory can be coaxed out of the arid soil of Zionist slogans—becomes necessary. We may be reluctant to give account of ourselves, knowing that such an account would be riddled with contradiction. But the Zionist cannot be reluctant.

What can such a theory be built of? No Zionism can ask itself to deny the importance of taking up life in the Jewish State. None can speak of a central point other than Jerusalem. Any Zionist theory which purports to deem Shaker Heights or Glencoe, Beverly Hills or Newton, as standing on the same elevated plane as Rishon LeZion ("The First to Zion"), Petach Tikvah ("Gate of Hope"), or Mevasseret Zion ("Harbinger of Zion") cannot be taken seriously. There are givens, and the givens define the unacceptable, the ludicrous.

Nor will Zionism as an expression of utopian ethnic loyalty suffice. Zionism without Zion is simply not possible. Which brings us back to locative Zionism, to Zionism as place. But a Zionism that is wholly locative, that points solely to emigration and that repeats continually slogans about a centrality that everyone concedes but no one perceives, is not a useful Zionism. So these are the boundaries of the problem: On the one hand, we have utopian Zionism, which is a contradiction, and on the other hand, we have locative Zionism, which is an obstacle.

A solution? But I have already cautioned that I have none. I know only that American Jewry lives a life that is separated from reality by a veil. American Judaism offers a life that is centrally constructed around symbols of other times and of other places. In Israel, Jewish life is concrete and unmediated; that life is in dramatic contrast to ours, which is a life of compromise, of self-restraint, of small self-deceptions and of petty pretense. The myth of "Holocaust and Redemption" accurately describes and evokes the everyday world of Israeli Jews, who day by day confront the possibility of their own destruction in very real ways, and who day by day take steps to defend against it. The myth makes sense over there, all the more so because it is not an exclusive myth, because there are other components to the Israeli myth-system. But here? What reality does the myth conjure? What response do the symbols of death and of triumph over death evoke for a people who know a world of exile very much like the world that was once destroyed—but who have formed no other world for themselves?

The infinitely depressing conclusion is that American Judaism is founded upon the living of life through the lives of other people, some of whom were slaughtered, others of whom prevailed. Our Judaism is a spectator sport; we sit before the screen and watch how it was done long ago, how it is done today—elsewhere. We are the ones who never exercise, but who will never fail to watch the game. Our sport is neither exercise nor even fun; it is simply spectacle. What we understand as Jews is that we are to love with a breaking heart, that we are to hold close with open arms. We cannot turn off the set; we would not know what to do with ourselves or what to make of ourselves were the screen to go blank. But we cannot do more than watch.

Part Three

Golah and Zion

9. Can We Be Zionists?

Some Israelis claim we American Jews are not and cannot be Zionists—that American Jewry is a dying, disintegrating community, that our only hope as Jews is to settle in the Jewish State. I deny those assertions.

I think it is time to hear some good things about American Jewry today and tomorrow. I think it is time for the realists, let alone the optimists, to have their say.

First, we are a very young community, no more than eighty years old in our present form. The institutions and organizations, the forms of Jewish expression, the national religious movements—none of these goes back much before 1870, and the communal structures we have built are much more recent than that. I think it is too soon to despair of the great structures of American Jewry; we have accomplished much in a brief time, and we do not know how the fifth and sixth generations of American Jewry will do.

Second, it is not only too soon to despair, but it is time to take confidence in what we have already produced. We have now produced a third and a fourth generation of American Jews who *choose* to be Jews.

Judaism, so long protected by the hostility of the outside world, today faces the challenges of a free society and meets those challenges. We know that is so because we see resources of Jewish commitment and Jewish devotion in young people, who are not nostalgic or guilty toward the past but eager for

79

the future. Fifty years ago you could not have taken for granted there would be even one more generation of American Jews.

In the 1920's and 30's Jewry suffered a great hemorrhage, a bleeding of resources, loyalties, commitments. Jews thought then that the choice was to be an American or to be a Jew, and being Jewish was seen to be parochial, narrow, particular, while being American was perceived as broad, open-minded, and universal. Jewish education was ignored, so that hundreds of thousands of American Jews perceived Judaism from the public stage or the public press, but not from the spiritual resources of Judaism itself. Jewish observance was at a low ebb. Traditionalism in all its forms was written off as "un-American."

Now turn around and look at the young Jews of the seventies (and eighties). They are more Jewish than their parents. As Jews they are, if not well-educated, at least better educated. They know more Hebrew. They want to learn more about Jewish tradition and they want to practice it.

Come to the university campus with me, and look at the students I see, not one by one, but in platoons and regiments. They are intensely serious about being Jewish. To be sure, they express their interests differently from their parents—who not infrequently object to their undertaking academic Jewish studies to begin with.

Where did the movement to free Soviet Jewry find its most profound response, if not on the campus? Where is the constant struggle with Arab propaganda able to draw upon the richest resources of Jewish talent, if not among the Jewish professors and students? Where is Jewish education taken seriously, if not on the campus? I take pride in the homes and parents who produced my students. Ladies of Hadassah: You are, as parents, among the great generations of Jewish mothers, for your children are better Jews than you are, and you made them so.

So enough of the despair and the disillusion. You have proved beyond doubt that there *can* be Judaism in America, that we *can* nurture the loyalties of young Jews whose experience is wholly within our Jewish community and within American society. That fact was much in doubt fifty years ago. It is in no doubt whatsoever today. I for one am sated with talk of the "vanishing American Jew." I think he is here to stay—and so is she.

Obviously we have problems. We rightly worry about intermarriage. We should worry more than we do about indifference and apathy and about the depth of Jewish education. We have yet to achieve the piety and faith that alone will sustain our lives.

But the issue is not whether we have already achieved the Garden of Eden. The issue is whether we should despair of our future.

I have no better argument for the promise of our future as a community than Hadassah itself, sixty years old and hundreds of thousands of women strong! Who in 1912 would have had the vision of what you have become in 1972? Those who then despaired had a good case. Jews in large numbers were leaving the Jewish community as fast as they could; Jewishness was old, it was greenhorn, it was ignoble. Forget Yiddish and Hebrew. Forget the Jewish people. Become Americans. And Zion? Who wants to hear about Zion? But those who then refused to despair had a better case: We shall not give up hope in the human resources of American Jewry, in the Jewish loyalties of the coming generations.

I today say the same thing, for my students have shown me what I could not have hoped for in their parents—a Jewish student generation with a serious commitment to Judaism. So I affirm that we American Jews form a stable community, capable of meeting all its problems and solving some of them; a community responsive to new challenges, a community capable of orderly change.

What of the second issue before us: Can we be Zionists in America? Or are those Israelis right who claim that to be a Zionist is to settle in the Land of Israel? Obviously, the answer depends upon what you mean by Zionism.

Let me give my view of Zionism.

The Jewish People is my homeland. Wherever Jews live, there I am at home. And Zionism is the highest expression of the Jewish People's will to endure. I am a Zionist because I am a Jew; Zionism is integral to Judaism as I understand it. These words are not unfamiliar. In one way or another we repeat them every day. But their meaning and implications have to be searched out.

When I say that the Jewish People is my homeland, I am affirming Jewish peoplehood. Zionism asserts that Jews are a people that wishes to survive and to enrich its spiritual life. In the words of Mordecai M. Kaplan: "Zionism has been defined as 'that movement in Jewish life which seeks to foster a capacity among Jews for the living of a more abundant Jewish life.' " Zionism is the means by which the Jewish People has sought "to survive and to remain true to its destiny . . . Zionism is contemporary Judaism in action." Therefore "Zionism should treat the establishment of the State of Israel only as the first indispensable step in the salvaging of the Jewish people and the regeneration of its spirit." (*A New Zionism.* New York, 1935, Theodor Herzl Foundation, p. 27)

In short, we are *Zionists because we are Jews.* Zionism is integral to our understanding of Judaism. This goes back to the third plank in the Basel Program of 1897: "To strengthen Jewish sentiment and national self-consciousness." This is the only unrealized part of the program. The others—"to promote the settlement in Palestine of Jewish workers, to centralize the Jewish People by means of general institutions conformable to the laws of the land, and to obtain the sanctions of government necessary for carrying out the objects of Zionism"—have all been realized in the creation of the State of Israel, the Jewish Agency, the World Zionist Congress, and the like. But who would say that hopes to strengthen "Jewish sentiment and national self-consciousness" have reached the same high degree of fulfillment as the others? The contrary is the case, as everyone knows.

The Zionist task of the hour is to carry out that third principle of Basel. Accordingly, "Zionism will be judged by its efforts for Jewish survival more than by its efforts in behalf of [the State of] Israel . . . No less than our obligation to see Israel through its difficult period is our obligation to defeat indifference, arrest assimilation, combat disintegration, for these dangers are more imminent today than in any previous period in our history." So stated Nahum Goldmann at the first American Zionist Assembly (December 5, 1953).

Now the issue is raised, can one be a Jew or a Zionist in America or Canada? I am embarrassed to raise that issue before the ladies of Hadassah. For sixty years Hadassah was never interested in that debate. Henrietta Szold wrote, "Every day I face my daily crisis." It was in that spirit that Hadassah faced the little tempest of last winter. Professor Moshe Davis of the Hebrew University wrote to me at that time: "The ladies of the Congress remained ladies. They went back to the hotel, had a good cry, and then one of them said, 'Girls, let's go to sleep. Tomorrow we start again.' That's why Hadassah is synonymous with Jewish heart and soul."

As a matter of fact, I do not think a single Israeli in need stayed away from the Hadassah hospital in Jerusalem the next morning. No one boycotted Hadassah clinics or stayed out of the Vocational School. The argument is just that, an *argument* not worth much time—unless it affects your morale. Hadassah has been too busy with the daily crisis to concern itself with a few roughneck ideologues. Yet, I fear the issue affects morale and therefore may impede our confrontation with the daily crisis. That is why we have to discuss it.

What is the viewpoint of the other side? It goes like this: The Jews constitute a nation, and that nation is the State of Israel. Therefore to be a Zionist is to participate in Israeli nationality and nationalism, to live in the State of Israel. As to Judaism, it is a religion and stands apart from Zionism. Judaism as a religion served a good purpose in preserving the Jews in the exile; its remnants persist in Israeli society, to be sure, but no one not "religious" in the Israeli sense is expected to take Judaism seriously. Who has not been told by young Israelis, "We are not Jews. We are Israelis!"?

The issue before us is whether or not to affirm the *golah* as an integral part of the Jewish world, as an equal partner, with the State of Israel, in the Zionist enterprise. But the larger issue, given our definition of Zionism, is whether we American Zionists have a portion and a place in the Land of Israel, and whether we have a part in Judaism. If Zionism is integral to Judaism and we cannot be Zionists, how can we regard ourselves as good Jews?

There is no middle, no compromise. Either we American Zionists have an equal place in the Zionist movement or we do not. Either it is legitimate for us as Zionists to pursue our own Jewish goals or it is not. The third position—that we can be Jews without Zionism—is closed to us. World Jewry no longer wants to debate the existence or desirability of the Jewish State. We now are all Zionists.

We do not have to give serious effort to talk only in terms of whether or not we can make a living in Israel, or whether life in America is better or worse than life in Israel. Individual preferences for a cool climate over a hot one are trivial and not pertinent to the issue. Nor are we required to claim in America's or Canada's or Britain's behalf that society is perfect and the Jews' position wholly favorable. We shall not allege that Washington or Ottawa is our Jerusalem. The opposite is the case. What we claim is that Jerusalem is *our* Jerusalem too.

Instead of debating whether a Zionist must live in the State of Israel, I think we had best focus discussion with Israeli Zionists on a more constructive issue. It is how to define the relationship between Zionists in various parts of the world and in the State of Israel. I hope that relationship will be marked by reciprocity, mutual respect, good will, the capacity to differ in realistic mutual understanding.

First, we must recognize that that relationship provides enormous benefits to our own community. In important ways the State of Israel does for us things we cannot do for ourselves. Its society explores the potentialities of Jewishness, not to mention of the Judaic inheritance, in ways which are closed to us.

At the same time the achievements of the State of Israel give pride to world Jewry, with our community at its head. Its accomplishments as a society and its capacity for social, cultural and political greatness attest to the character of the whole Jewish People. If all Israel stand as pledges for one another, then the State of Israel is the rightful guarantor of our good name in the world.

Second, we perceive that, just as we need the State of Israel and constant, close relationships with Israeli life, so the State of Israel and its social and cultural life benefit from the ties with American Jewry. The relationship is entirely mutual and wholly reciprocal. We are their equals, as they are ours, and we can accept no other definition of the relationship.

On the material side, let us not evade the fact that now, and for some time to come, the State of Israel requires the support of the diaspora communities, American Jewry most of all. So in a worldly way, we need the State of Israel for the benefit of our own community and the Israelis need us for their interest as well.

But that relationship does not exhaust the spiritual potential of either party. For world Jewry, in important ways, the State of Israel constitutes the spiritual center, just as Ahad Haam said it should a long time ago.

What are these ways? The State of Israel is the greatest Jewish educational resource at hand. For us it is a classroom in Jewish living and in living Judaism, a classroom without walls. There is the best place to learn the meaning of the Sabbath. There is the place to recover our roots in our own past, the past of the Hebrew Bible and the Talmud, and to continue the struggle to interpret the Torah and apply it to changing life.

The State of Israel has become the spiritual center for world Jewry because it plays a decisive and central role in the Jewish mind and imagination, in shaping the Jewish identity and in the revival of the Jewish spirit in the present generation.

But in some important ways, even Zionism is not enough, for it is part, not all, of Judaism.

Today, Judaism is subordinated to Zionism, while in the

past, Zionism grew out of Judaism. Many suppose that being Jewish means only worldly action in behalf of the State of Israel and Jews who need to go there. But I argue the contrary: being a Zionist means spiritual involvement with the Judaic tradition that underlies Zionism, that forms the Jewish People and gives meaning to its existence, purpose to its endeavors, hope to its future.

In a profound sense, those who demand aliyah are saying something important: it is not enough to give your money, you have to give your soul, your self. Practically speaking, they are telling us there is something to Zionism, and to Jewishness, which should occupy our lives during all the time that we are not giving and raising money for the State of Israel. To those who speak of aliyah in those terms, I say yes, aliyah is a great *mitsvah*.

But there are other *mitsvot*: so many that not all of us can do them all, but none of us is exempt from doing some. To the American Jew who wants to hear only about the State of Israel I say, Zionism has more to say to you than that; it stands for more than letters to congressmen or checks to campaigns. And our ties to the State of Israel are deeper, far deeper, than political. We are one people, wherever we live. We stand before one Torah, wherever we are. We have much to do, whatever Jewish task we undertake.

Enough of the extremism which sets all value on one task, when we have many tasks and many responsibilities. Our problem now is how to be a Jew. Whoever can help us answer that question, show us how to explore the potentialities of Jewish Peoplehood—such a person is the sage of our time.

For us as for the Israelis, therefore, there can be one common spiritual center only, and that is the Judaic tradition, which for centuries has made manifest its capacity to define and to ennoble—to sanctify—the Jewish condition under every circumstance. It is the Judaic tradition which speaks to the eternal issues of death and life, which asks questions about the purpose and meaning of existence, and which gives answers to those questions. The Judaic tradition imparts meaning to the tears and anguish of the ordinary man.

Judaism takes that ordinary people and shows them to be part of an extraordinary people, links them to its past and assigns them a place in its destiny, grasps hold of their private time and joins it to a rhythm of eternity. And that Judaic tradition, mediated by experience unique to a given situation, is variously realized under all circumstances and with equal authenticity—in the *golah* or in the Holy Land alike. We seek large and general meanings for our small and highly particular lives. That search leads to, and within, Judaism.

10. American Jewry and The State of Israel: Toward a Mature Relationship

A mature relationship among adults is marked by reciprocity, mutual respect and good will, capacity to differ without rancor, and above all, mutual understanding. Mature men and women perceive one another without fantasy—either a fantastic dream or a fantastic nightmare about the other. By these standards, how shall we characterize the relationship between American Jewry and the State of Israel?

Two events of the current year suggest that the relationship between the largest Jewish community in the world, on the one side, and the most influential Jewish community in the world, on the other, is not mature.

First, on the Israeli side: One can only regard as disgraceful the treatment of the diaspora Zionists at the World Zionist Congress. Dr. Nahum Goldmann said that Soviet Jews should have not only the right to emigrate, but also the right to live as Jews in the USSR. What he asked for was what American Jews take for granted for themselves. For such a heresy—which undoubtedly is shared by the whole of thinking American Jewry—he was unceremoniously thrown off the agendum of the World Zionist Congress. No one pretended other than that a "dissenter" from the official line was unwelcome. What was puzzling, at the time, was the failure of the World Zionist Congress officials even to pretend that something other than the brutal, naked suppression of dissenting opinion was at hand. They were not even embarrassed.

Had anyone imagined that the attack on free speech was a temporary aberration, he was soon brought back to reality. The ladies of Hadassah found out otherwise. They opposed a resolution which, in effect, declared that Zionism consists solely of 'aliyah: Zionist leadership in the diaspora must be in the hands only of those who are in the last stages prior to emigration. The implication of that resolution is simply this: The Golah-communities have no share in Zion. Only those who live in the land of Israel may regard themselves as Zionists; the rest are outsiders, second-class citizens in the world Jewish community. When, moreover, the Hadassah delegation dramatized its protest by leaving the hall, the other side showered upon our ladies a torrent of abuse, according to newspaper reports, including profanity.

Now say what you will about Hadassah—and I cannot think of a valid criticism of that organization—you cannot justify abuse, profanity, unrestrainedly violent language, against those women! Theirs is a whole, mature, and self-sacrificing Zionist commitment. They are not the narrow, "Israel-only" people. They are Jews, whose Jewishness leads to a deep commitment to Zion and to Zionism, as much as to a serious involvement with Judaism. They are not a bowling league with a Jewish name. They are not tin-horn politicians using their Jewishness to gain attention they otherwise would not get. They are not "check-book Jews," whose Jewish commitment is fulfilled in giving money. They raise funds for purposes they fully understand. Their programs of study, both of contemporary Near Eastern realities and of Judaism, are serious and solid. They stand for, they embody, the best qualities of American Jewry.

These two incidents—the unashamed use of power to silence expression of an alterntive viewpoint, the unrestrained attack on our best and most devoted leadership—suggest that on the Israeli side, something is out of kilter. What sort of a relationship involves the refusal to hear a conflicting opinion? Who throws a temper-tantrum when frustrated? I should claim that in both incidents, the Israeli leadership acted in a childish way. Who but a child has not the patience to contend with disagreement, but prefers to close his ears? Who but a child throws a temper-tantrum when faced with measured opposition? So the Israeli side of the relationship between the two great Jewries is puerile. They act like spoiled children, who have been indulged so long and so mindlessly, and been faced with so little self-respect and dignity on the other side, that childish tactics are deemed normal.

But who can claim that, on the American Jewish side, we enter into mature and adult relationships with Israel? On the contrary, if the Israelis act like spoiled children, we behave like spoiled, indulgent parents. Look at our parental record: Irresponsible indulgence, along with preoccupied, self-centered indifference. We have been the models of the bad father and mother, who give the child everything he needs—but the one thing he wants, which is serious involvement. We give money, but pretend we want nothing for it and claim we get no return. So the Israelis are turned into our clients, children beholden to our largesse. We come in droves, to see what we want to see, not to learn about reality and to share in the burdens of real life. We come like lady-bountiful, with her basket of canned peaches for Thanksgiving, and her message of good cheer to the miserable masses. Given the blood and suffering, the deprivation and struggle which goes into the creation of the State of Israel and into the maintenance of its security, the building of its economy, and the creation of its society and culture, we have given nothing. The child has raised himself. The parent has given little more than excess cash, pocket-money.

For what we want for our money is more than a good conscience. We pay not merely a ransom for our absent bodies. We purchase a fantasy—and are not satisfied with the real achievements of the real Israel. What is that fantasy? To understand what we dream, you have to know what we have known as mundane life. What are the components of the everyday imagination of the mature American Jew.

He is the child of outsiders, of immigrants. If he came to maturity in the late 1920s, making a living was a terrible struggle, a struggle complicated by being a Jew. Whole professions and industries were closed to him. In the 1930s and 1940s being a Jew was not merely an economic handicap, but a psychological disaster. It meant living in a world where the accident of birth imposed a sentence of death. Who could close his ears to the anti-Semitism of the radio? Who could close his eyes to the debates in the public press about whether the Jews were a good thing or a bad thing? About whether the Jewish people should live or die? About whether the Jewish community should continue to maintain its heritage or should vote, all at once and unanimously, to disintegrate?

When, in the late 1930s and afterward, a visa was a matter of life and death, the western democracies were hardly generous in granting life. Who can forget the "joke" about the German Jew at the travel agency seeking a way out of Germany. The agent got out the globe, and pointed to country after country where Jews were not admitted. Soon it appeared that the whole world was closed. So the Jew asked, "Herr Travel Agent, this globe is evidently no good. Don't you have another world?" The whole of today's Jewish leadership either remembers those awful days or endured them. We remember the refugee ships, steaming from port to port, looking for a place willing to receive their unwanted human cargo. In our dreams, who does not sail in such ships night by night? And we remember the concentration camps and the death-chambers and crematoria, the hills of gold fillings, the two million pairs of children's shoes, a pathetic mountain reaching up to the skies? Who can forget them? Who for all the rest of Jewish history will not some night awake out of the nightmare that he is there, his children there, his mother and father there.

How does the nightmare of our childhood or youth relate to the State of Israel? What connection does it have to our present dilemma? The answer is: the creation of the State of Israel and its subsequent achievements replaced a ghastly nightmare with a beautiful vision. And it did more—though it would have been enough—than to give pride to the ashamed and hope to the despairing. The creation of the State of Israel lent meaning and significance to all that had gone before. The suffering and the horror were not without meaning. The dark night was prelude to the great light. All that had happened and had been endured was not in vain. The murder of many people was not simply a massacre. It was a Holocaust. The creation of another nation-state in the Levant was not merely a political event. It was the beginning of redemption.

This constitutes the myth that gives meaning and transcendence to the petty lives of ordinary people—the sacred story of darkness followed by light, the story of a passage through the netherworld and past the gates of hell, then, purified by suffering and blood, the rebirth into the new age. Such is the structure of the classic myth of a salvific religion: the story of sin and atonement, disaster and redemption, salvation and a new heaven and a new earth—the passing away of former things. This story invests ordinary, everyday events with transcendent significance and supernatural importance. It is this story which shapes the mind and imagination of American Jewry and supplies the correct interpretation of mundane events. It turns workday people into saints. It transforms commonplace affairs into *history* and turns writing a check into a sacred act.

What is wrong with such a story? Why call it a "myth"? Is it not true? To be sure, in our guts we know this is how things really were, and what they really meant. But we know it because the myth of suffering and redemption corresponds to our perceptions of reality, evokes immediate recognition and assent. It not only bears meaning, it imparts meaning precisely because it explains experience and derives from what we know to be true.

But one must ask whether experience is so stable, the world so unchanging, that we may continue to explain today's reality in terms of what happened yesterday. The answer is that, much as we might want to, we cannot. The world has moved on. We can remember, but we cannot reenact what happened. We cannot replicate the experiences which required explanation according to a profound account of the human and the

Jewish condition. We cannot, because our children will not allow it. They experience a different world—perhaps not better, perhaps not so simple, but certainly different. They know about events, but have not experienced them. And what they know they perceive through their experience of a very different world. The story that gives meaning and imparts transcendence to the everyday experiences of being Jewish simply does not correspond to the reality of the generations born since 1945. They did not know the frightful insecurity, did not face the meaninglessness of Jewish suffering, therefore cannot appreciate the salvation that dawned with the creation of the State of Israel.

That does not mean the coming generations cannot appreciate Zion and cannot establish in their own lives an important place for the State of Israel. They can and they will. But it cannot be a place made vacant by unperceived reality and unfelt experience. They have not known a world without the State of Israel. They have not faced the degrading and humiliating experiences of the 1920's and 30's and 40's. Our problems are not their problems. Our nightmares are not theirs. And we cannot endow their imagination with our dreams.

Theirs is a more complicated world. Not for them the simple choice of death or life, the simple encounter with uncomplicated evil. For them Jewishness also is more complicated, for, while the world of the 1930's and 1940's imparted a "Jewish education," and a "Jewish consciousness" was elicited by reading a newspaper or simply encountering a hostile society, today's world does not constitute a school without walls for the education of the Jews. That is, I think, a good thing. Being Jewish no longer is imposed by negative experiences, but is now called forth by affirmative ones. For the younger generation the State of Israel stands not as the end of despair but as the beginning of hope. It enriches the choices facing the young Jew and expands his consciousness of the potentialities of Jewishness. Not its existence, but its complexity is important. Not its perfection, but its imperfection is compelling. It is important as the object not of fantasy, but of perceived reality.

A whole new relationship is called for—a relationship between the healthy and the healthy, not between the frightened and the saving remnant of a doomed world. The fathers, there and here, could not stand too much reality. They were paralyzed by the past and immobilized in the fear that present reality might not, in the end, compensate for horror. So they demanded perfection. On the American Jewish side, that meant seeing what was not, what could not be there. On the Israeli side it meant pandering to that vision by turning pilgrims into tourists and spreading before them a stage-set peopled by handsome heroes, unreal stage-actors. A visit to the Land of Israel was supposed, on both sides, to be an extended stay in the local movie-house, a long sitting before a television set.

So we needed a prolonged fantasy, and, whether cynically or sincerely, the Israelis gave it to us. Or, more accurately, they sold it, but at an enormous cost to themselves and to us. They paid in self-respect. They understood that they were not loved for what they were. So what they were was not enough, was inadequate. Degraded by our perception, they hated us. The hatred became all the more intense because they needed us. We were the indulgent father, interested only in the good appearance of the child, not in his even better reality. We were concerned—oh, how we were concerned!—that the child should live and be well. But without us. Without our real involvement and serious concern with all that he really was and really accomplished. That was too much.

And we paid a price, perhaps higher than the Israelis, for our fantasy. We lied to ourselves. Our self-deceit consisted in the claim that we really cared about something to which, in our hearts, we were essentially indifferent. On the one side, we said to ourselves, "Everything for them. Nothing for ourselves." So we lavished our material resources on the object of our fantasy, and failed to nurture our own spiritual resources. But in acting out the little playlet of the indulgent father who gives the child everything he has but nothing of himself, we deprived ourselves of something so precious as to defy a price: a true relationship with real people, a deep involvement with the flesh-and-blood realities. We never really knew those far-off "children" whose bills we paid (we thought) and to whom we sent expensive toys.

All that they could have given us was inadequate to compensate for what we really wanted, which was an unreal vision—of *ourselves*. For the Israelis had to be everything we were not; they had to achieve goals we knew we never could meet. We saw ourselves as citified and soft. They had to be hard and strong. We saw ourselves as weak and craven. They had to be brave and courageous. We saw ourselves as pariahs, without roots and without a home. They had to put down roots and build for us a homeland we really did not want or need, except at night, in the fearful dreams of dawn. Above all, we saw ourselves as not really Jewish, as having compromised with American or with Western culture. So they had to be Jewish, and not only Jewish, but religious in a way we never should accept for ourselves.

So the "fathers" turned themselves into children—of their dependents. They had, it turned out, nothing to give the children—no model of maturity, no strength, no source of dignity and self-respect. They gave the children their money, because it was all they had. The children took that money, thinking it was all they wanted. What a sad family! How melancholy its fate—the father indulging the child because he had nothing more to give, but demanding from the child something no one can rightly ask; the child taking from the father with contempt, asking from the father that he become exactly like the child (so the petulant and deamaning spirit in which they speak of *'aliyah*).

But the family of which I speak is the House of Israel, the Jewish people, a family with long memories and a fundamentally sound psychic history. Somehow the fathers, for all their failure and frailty, manage to bring up children as different from themselves as is father from son. The children indeed differ in every respect except the important one. On our side, the reality of the State of Israel turns out to fascinate the younger generation still more than the fantasy mesmerized the fathers. If the 1950's and 1960's were times in which the State of Israel rose to the top of the agendum of American Jewry, in the 1970's (and 1980's) it seems to constitute the whole of the agendum. No other Jewish issue has the power to engage the younger generation of Jews as does the issue of the State of Israel. But Israelism—involvement with the State of Israel without commitment to the ideologies of Zionism or to Judaism—seems to me not a matter of fantasy for the younger generation. The relationship they seek is not of the patron to the servile or of the indulgent disinterested parent to the scheming, unhappy child. They seek not only to know, but, because they know, to participate in the realities of Israeli life. Of them one need not demand 'aliyah. They go because they want to. Their 'aliyah is not only a brief visit, but as a student or as a worker. Many choose to settle. Many more, deciding not to settle for personal reasons, feel no need to turn private choices into a public ideology, an ideology of the glorious, cultured, world-serving diaspora, as against the straitened, parochial, self-serving homeland. Anti-Zionism and anti-Israelism are virtually non-existent among the new generation of Jews. (Those on the fringes are not interesting in the present context.) That is to say, whether or not there should be a State of Israel, why there should be such a State, how one must justify the existence of a Jewish state in terms of a higher morality or claim in its behalf that it is a light to the nations—these modes of thought are simply alien. The State of Israel *is.* The issue for the younger generation is not, is it a good thing or a bad thing? The issue is, since we know no other world but one in which the State of Israel is present, how shall we relate to that important part of the world in which we live?

The younger generation exhibits a healthier relationship to the State of Israel than did the fathers, not because it is more virtuous (despite its fantasies), but because it has not had to live through the frightening, sickening experiences of the fathers. If the myth of the fathers is irrelevant to the children, and if the fantasy-ridden relationships of the fathers are not replicated by the children, the reason is that the young people have grown up in a healthier world. It is a world not without its nightmares, but with different, less terrifying nightmares for the Jews in particular. In days gone by, the "Jewish problem" belonged to Jews alone. Whether we lived or died was our problem. But now the problem of life or death faces all mankind; we are no longer singled out for extermination. The terror is everyone's. If there is a just God, a mark of God's justice is that those who did not share our anguish must now share our nightmares, an exact, if slow, measure of justice. We who saw ourselves all alone in the death camps have been joined by the rest of the world. Next time fire instead of gas, perhaps. But meanwhile it is an easier life.

Nor should we ignore the fact that for the younger generation, being Jewish has conferred the practical advantages of a group capable of mutual protection in a generally undifferentiated society. It has been a positive advantage in the recent past. Add to this the devotion of the Jewish parent to the Jewish child. Jewish children are treated in Jewish homes as very special beings. This makes young Jews strive to excel in the rest of society as they did at home. To be sure, this produces a large crop of Jewish adults who blame their Jewishness for the fact that the rest of society does not treat them as did their parents. These are people who need evidence to explain what they see as their own failure, which is actually explicable by their own impossible demands on themselves and on society. Being Jewish in the recent past in the balance has been an advantage, rather than a disability. The younger generation is better off on that account.

The relationship between the new generation of American Jews and the new generation of Israelis therefore may prove healthier and more stable than that of the past generation. I hope it will be marked by reciprocity, mutual respect, good will, the capacity to differ with good will, and realistic mutual understanding. To be sure, we on our part cannot describe the Israeli perception of the relationship, nor can we tell the other side how to carry on its part. But we can and should reflect upon our perception of the relationship and spell out for ourselves the potential we perceive.

The State of Israel has become the spiritual center for world

Jewry because it plays a decisive and central role in the Jewish mind and imagination, in shaping the Jewish identity, and in the revival of the Jewish spirit in the present, not only the past, generation. Why the young people should respond as did their fathers to the existence of the State of Israel I cannot say, for, as I suggested, their experience as Jews greatly differs from that of the earlier generation. But there can be no doubt of the facts. In their Jewishly-oriented activism, in their interest in Hebrew language and Jewish culture, the effect of the State of Israel on the present young generation of the diaspora has been deeply spiritual, not merely material. It probably will be more important to American Jewry's spiritual life in the next generation than it is today, as the spiritual resources of American Jewry continue to diminish.

But in some important ways the State of Israel cannot serve as American Jews' 'spiritual center' and never could. For being Jewish constitutes not merely a national or ethnic, cultural and social experience. It also is meant to supply an orientation toward life, a mode of being human, a perspective on humanity on history, on what it means to die and to live. And those aspects of being Jewish which pertain to the nature of human existence cannot be wholly separated from the particularities of everyday life: the actual, concrete situation in which one *is* Jewish. Our perception of ourselves and of the world and the meaning of life begins in our own situation, and that is a complex one. For our lives are shaped by the experience of being Jewish and being something else, many other things. We are not wholly Jewish. Our values are derived from sources other than solely Jewish or Judaic ones. Our perception of life encompasses a society quite different from that of the State of Israel. Our search for abiding values takes place in a personal and cultural setting in important ways unlike that of the State of Israel. The life for which we seek meaning, for good or ill, is a life in the *Golah*, a life in two civilizations. And we are marginal in our situation. The Israelis are at home in theirs. We are in a measure alien; they are never strangers. They perceive reality close at hand. Our perceptions are one stage removed from the center of things. For us the given is something to be criticized and elevated, for we do not take perceived reality at face value. For them things are very different. At the very center of our being is an experience unavailable to the Israeli, and the contrary is also the case. Theirs is the right to criticize us and question our perpetuation of marginality. But we have made our choices, for ourselves and our children.

For us as for the Israelis there can be one common spiritual center only, and that is the Judaic tradition, which for centuries has made manifest its capacity to define and to ennoble—to sanctify—the Jewish condition under every circumstance. It is the Judaic tradition which speaks to the eternal issues of death and life, which asks questions about the purpose and meaning of existence, and which gives answers to those questions. The Judaic tradition imparts meaning to the tears and anguish of the ordinary person, gives to life transcendence, lends purpose to what seems purposeless—living and dying. Judaism takes ordinary persons and shows them to be part of an extraordinary people, links them to its past and assigns them a place in its destiny, grasps hold of their private time and joins it to a rhythm of eternity, links their mortal being to the natural course of the seasons and of life itself, distinguishes one day from the next and one deed from the next. And that Judaic tradition, mediated by experience unique to a given situation, is variously realized under all circumstances and with equal authenticity—in the *Golah* or in the holy land alike.

11. "We" and "They"— or One People?

One thing I think most American Jews take for granted: the American Jewish community is here to stay. Barring a calamity we do not now foresee, there will be Jews in America for a very long time; these Jews will probably want to come together and so form a community of some sort. I think that self-under-standing and self-acceptance come to Israelis as a considerable surprise. For they are not always too polite to remind us of the fate of European Jewry. They are not invariably too tactful to ask us how we can remain in *golah,* not from the viewpoint of our spiritual welfare (though they take for granted as Jews we should "go on welfare" of the spirit), but from the viewpoint of our very physical survival.

Just now M. Z. Frank berates me in the National Jewish Post for ignoring the dismal history of European Jewry. What is there to reply? If you predict that some day something will happen and you wait long enough, it probably will happen, because anything is possible. But that may be long, long in the future, and many things can happen in-between. Would a Polish Jew of the twelfth century have been ill-advised to settle in Lublin? But would a Polish Jew of 1937 have been ill-advised to leave? We cannot claim "it" will never, can never happen here. Anything can happen anywhere. Physical security is relative, though, and sometimes accidental. Just now I learned in Howard Sacher's brilliant book, *Europe Leaves the Middle East,*

100

that the British fully expected Rommel to advance on Suez, and their next line of defense was to be in front of Haifa. But for a few accidents of war, the *Yishuv* would have suffered a terrible fate. Should we then have thought Zionism somehow proved by history to be "wrong"? Unless you believe in a God who governs the most concrete and specific events of history (and Judaism has always taught belief in such a God), you had better not claim "history proves" one thing or another, the rightness, or the wrongness, of any particular choice. You can never be sure you are wrong to predict that something *will* happen. But you are bound to be wrong if you predict that something will *not* happen.

I do not know what will happen to our community. I know only that for me and I hope for my children, this is where I propose to live. This is the society whose problems are my problems. In the Talmud there is a story of two sages who find a dreadful village, in which the flies are so large as to threaten the lives of children. But the people praise the pleasures of living in their town. The sages say, "Blessed is he who made this place charming for the people who live here." Can our brethren in Israel not find the tolerance to say so of us? For the vast majority of our community seems to have decided here to remain, and many of those who have settled in Israel eventually return. I do not claim that is a wonderful thing, but I am not persuaded it is to be condemned either. Why should we either praise or condemn the myriad private decisions of individuals? Is it our place to judge where people live? Is it not our task to help them, wherever they live, to conduct life in accord with the ideals of Torah?

The issues of Torah pertain to men and women wherever they are. What are the questions before us? They concern the purpose and meaning of life, the way to conduct oneself in each setting of everyday affairs. Torah speaks of Israel, the Jewish people, and its way of consecrating its days and hallowing its years. The issues of Torah concern doing and obeying God's will as we are given to grasp it. True, the Torah was given in one particular place. But that is, in the wilderness—

nowhere. True, it is given to one particular people? But that is, to an *erev rav*, a mixed multitude, made by Torah into a *people*, Israel.

What is "being Jewish" to us? It begins in home and family. In this society we find ourselves, by choice more than by necessity, associated with others of common origin in European Jewry. What we make of that association is many things, or nothing. But for most of us we have to come to grips with "being Jewish." "Being Jewish" can mean gambling in Las Vegas and making movies in Hollywood, or it can mean pursuing great research in science and social studies; it can mean law or medicine. These all are things which disproportionately large numbers of Jews are supposed to do. "Being Jewish" can mean limiting one's choice of a mate or finding exogamy particularly attractive. My point is that "being Jewish" can mean nearly anything and its opposite. But as a religious Jew I do not concede it should mean just about everything. I want "being Jewish" to be synonymous with the man or the woman whom you can trust in the marketplace, to refer to someone who is considerate of another person's needs and feelings, to mean a person whose thoughts sometimes turn to God and who seeks in this life to conform to the laws and instructions in accord with which this world was made, reality was formed.

But whatever "being Jewish" should or should not mean, one thing it always does mean, and that is, being bound up with the fate of other Jews. That gambler in Las Vegas, that fat hedonist lying on the sand of Miami Beach, and all of us together cannot, however hard we try, ever dissociate ourselves from one another. The world will not permit. Nor will our religious tradition, our ethical heritage, our history—everything we stand for. As Professor Ben Halpern points out, every other definition of Judaism and explanation of Jewishness has been proved in modern times to be false. The one that stands the test of time and trial is this "Jewish Consensus": Jews are one people simply because what happens to one is felt by the other. They share an interdependence of fate. Or, to put it in religious terms, they share a common destiny: "Who has not made us like the nations of the earth and has not set our lot according to that of the families of land."

And since we are interdependent, we care very profoundly for what happens to our people wherever they live. We share very deeply in the achievements of our people. Who then will deny that the greatest achievement of the Jewish people in the two thousand years since the destruction of the Second Temple is the response to the Holocaust which culminated in May, 1948? The survivors of the Holocaust more than any other group stand behind the creation of the State of Israel. It was what they wanted, the only thing they wanted, and for a moment, the world listened to them. Reread the history of the years from 1933 to 1948. What you will learn is about those Jews who escaped with their lives alone, having lost not merely their property but their whole-world, their wives, their children, their brothers and sisters, their mothers and fathers, their all. Who would have blamed those people had they chosen to affirm the only life they had known those past six years, which was death. Who would have condemned them for saying, "No more, enough: We shall not be Jews again." Instead they said, "We shall be Jews in a Jewish state, we shall be a free people in our land, in the land of Zion and Jerusalem." They could have chosen death rather than rebuilding, suicide, moral disintegration, and some did. But the remnants of Israel in Europe chose instead to live and once more to integrate their lives, to marry, to build homes having lost homes, to have children having lost children. I do not know the source of moral courage and personal regeneration which at that dark hour gave new life to the people. But in their tens and hundreds of thousands, they gave birth to themselves again and so revived the entire Jewish people. Brands plucked from the burning, they rekindled the light of us all.

To me the State of Israel stands as the monument created by the survivors for the millions who perished, but even more as the testimony to the will of the Jewish people to endure, despite it all, *despite it all*. It represents here and now the eternity of Israel.

Yet in those same years American Jewry received survivors

too, and just as the *Yishuv* created a state, so we were not idle. This community too produced a new birth of Jewishness. The pathetic institutions of the pre-war period were re-created. The Jewish Theological Seminary went from a tiny enclave of faculty and students to become the center of a massive religious movement. Brandeis University came into being. The Reform movement saw the creation of hundreds of new synagogues, and these were not formed by escapees of Orthodoxy but by people who had turned their backs upon indifference and assimilation. Orthodoxy before World War II was a pitiful remnant. Afterward, through the efforts of both immigrants and native-born alike, Orthodoxy became a powerful force in American Jewry, with *yeshivot*, synagogues, day schools, an extraordinarily vital movement. If the State of Israel is twenty-five years old this year, I think American Jewry as we now know it is not much older. Much of what we now rely upon—our institutions, synagogues, Federations, but also our spiritual treasures—much of all this in its present form is not much more than a quarter-century-old.

To me the American Jewish community in its way stands as an affirmation of Jewish *life* against Jewish death on the part of people who see themselves as (and surely include among themselves) survivors of the millions who perished. We too testify to the will of the Jewish people to endure, despite it all. True, we stand in spite of the easy road out, we struggle not against physical hardship and through martial courage, but against the more difficult, less dramatic, surely less colorful trials of the human spirit. We defy not the laws of war, as did the Israelis in 1948, but the laws of sociology. How many groups have come to America, only to perish in the melting pot! But we have not perished. We have not lost our ties to our past and to our authentic being. We have suffered casualties and, alas, will have to endure many more. But we are here, and I think we shall continue for some time to come. I do not take this for granted. I find inexpressibly moving, ineffably beautiful, my students, so wholly and unselfconsciously American, so willingly and insouciantly Jewish. Fifty years ago you were the one or the other. Today a great many people, young and old alike, seek to be both, and yet one alone: to be themselves, wholly American and completely Jewish at one and the same time. That is not what they seek, but what they *are*.

Now it is in this context that we have to formulate a conception of ourselves in relationship to the State of Israel. As I said, I earlier tried to formulate matters in terms of Zionist theory. But this may be an error, for what is at issue in theory is not always made clear by theorizing. Zionist theory seems important to Israelis in explaining to themselves why they should stay in the land. That is why when they extend that theory to us they argue to be Zionists we must settle in the land, so to verify their doubting faith. But to us that is not a meaningful option. Then are we not Zionists?

Two exchanges in the recent past helped me clarify this matter. The first came in the aftermath of the Hadassah address, last August, when a prominent Israeli Hadassah leader said to Hadassah officers seated near me, "If Neusner is right, then why are we better than you are?" To which the Hadassah ladies replied, "For twenty-five years we've been trying to explain to you that we don't think you are better than we are!" The Israeli lady had taken for granted what the Americans had never for one moment perceived.

The second came in a letter from a close friend of mine, dean at an Israeli university and a fine scholar. I had reported to him the various exchanges on Zionism and sent him my papers. He has a fine sense of humor, and his reply was, "But Ya'aqov, surely you have to concede we are better *Israelis* than you are!"

Somewhere between these two stories I locate the central error in theorizing on Zionism: We are not Israelis at all: But we do not feel inferior in World Jewry. If this means we cannot regard ourselves as Zionists, so be it.

But so far as Zionism is the mode by which we express our enduring concern for the people, the land, and the State of Israel, so far as Zionism is the way in which, for our time and place, we give form to the yearning of our people for the land, to our prayers for its welfare, to our love of its hills and valleys, our faith in the bond between the land and the entire people of Israel—so far as Zionism is the contemporary expression of the Judaism which teaches us to seek the peace of Jerusalem, then, come what may, we are Zionists. And we are Zionists because we are Jews, because our understanding of Judaism leads us to Jerusalem, and not to Berlin, or London, or Washington, or even Borough Park.

The Israelis ought not to take for granted, furthermore, the importance of our commitment. They have enemies, even in the West, even in America. They cannot dismiss their friends as inferior. There is work to be done in their support. We are here to do it. Our communities send half of the voluntary taxes—the funds raised for Federations and Welfare Funds—to the U.J.A. for use in building the land of Israel. If we do not pay these taxes, who will? Our extra-Federation support for Israeli universities, centers of science and technology, synagogues and *yeshivot*, and countless other purposes, is hardly negligible. We buy their bonds and induce others to do so. If this does not make us Zionists, what are we then? Surely not Americans of the Mosaic persuasion, surely not anti-Zionists. I think a Zionist should be understood as someone who does the deeds required for Zion. We do a great many of them, even to the exclusion of projects necessary for our own future, and even to the neglect of our own community. If our fate or destiny is interdependent, we see ourselves as more dependent upon the Israelis than they possibly can see themselves dependent upon us.

Indeed, what happens there sometimes shakes us more than them. I recall that in 1970 Palestinians from Lebanon shelled a school bus and killed a number of little children. That day I met my friend, Yigael Yadin, then a visiting professor at Brown University. I could barely talk. He asked why, and I said I was grieving for the little children. He too was affected, but better able to carry on: "We live through such things." That is all he said. Again, in the awful days from May 15 to June 5, 1967, we relived the Holocaust. They prevented it. Whose lot was easier? Many now suppose that without the vitality of the State of

Israel, without its providing us with forms and substance for our Jewishness—however shallow, however trivial—the *Golah* could not sustain itself. I do not think that *has* to be so, but it is easy to concede it is the case. So, as I said, if we are interdependent, it is we who depend upon them.

But we do not regard ourselves as less authentic Jews or disloyal to the Jewish people because we love this country. We are different in our understanding of Jewishness from the Israelis. In some ways we are going to differ from them about what is important in Judaism. But at the crucial issue, the peoplehood of Israel, we do not differ. Like them we regard Jews as more than a random collection of individuals who happen to believe in the same theology. On the contrary, we deny the Jews are a religious group alone. We do not justify our situation by reference to a "mission of Israel" to the nations of the world, a mission best carried out by the dispersion of Israel among the nations. We do not offer a *golah*-nationalism as the counterpart to Israeli nationalism. The various nineteenth-century interpretations of the nature of Jewish peoplehood and the meaning of Jewish history are not going to be rehearsed by us. It does no good, therefore, to berate us for "anti-Zionism" or "non-Zionism" as if what those doctrines contain were pertinent to our thinking.

On the other hand, we do think the whole House of Israel, the Jewish people viewed as one people, should take a prudent view of its future. It probably was providential that, from 1933 to 1945, the entire Jewish people was not located in continental Europe. The more widely dispersed—within limits—the more likely we are to continue, whatever happens in one particular region of the world. The movement of Jewish history should have taught us that when the sun sets in one part of the Jewish world, it rises in another. *Lo alman Yisrael:* The Jewish people is not orphaned, it is subject to Providence. Nor is it wise to congregate wholly within one system of government or within a single power-bloc among the great nations: "Give a portion to seven, or even to eight, for you know not what evil may happen on earth." "In the morning sow your seed, and eat at evening withhold not your hand, for you do not know which will prosper, this or that, or whether both alike will be good." This is old wisdom. It still applies.

And we do think our community too has its contribution to make to the spiritual treasury of the House of Israel. The Israelis teach us what it means to respect oneself: they call us to dignity and confidence, give us pride despite ourselves. Their critique of the *Golah* and its subservient mentality, its time-serving and capacity to accommodate, is indispensable to our health. But will they not profit from our perspective, for we have learned good lessons too. Chief among them is the threat to human freedom and dignity posed by people who believe with perfect faith that whatever they do is right. The union of the state and the larger and transcendant values of life gives every bureaucrat the right to suppose he speaks in behalf of the Messiah. We have just gone through difficult times and have learned not to place confidence even in the best and brightest, in a measure to distrust all authority and all government. Israelis have yet to learn the dangers of excessive 'statism,' of devotion to the state as an end in itself. Can you imagine how Amos or Isaiah would laugh if someone told them Israel, the Jewish people, had set for itself the ideal of devotion to the state—any state, including its own?

We are dubious of all claims to justify whatever is expedient to the ruling party in terms of the security of the state, of unexamined, uncritical patriotism. And the Israelis may profit from our suspicion of that patriotism which consists in justifying what is expedient by appeals to the flag—even one with blue stripes and a six-pointed star.

Truly, there should be no "we" and no "they." We are not competing in a bridge tournament. "We American Jews" no more present a single front to the world, even to the Jewish world, than do "those Israelis." We are one family, one people, one House of Israel. We are varied as a people, and the various rooms in our household contain even more diverse individuals. But when confronted by claims of superiority and allegations of inferiority, and when these claims are made in terms of

Jewish Peoplehood or Judaism, then we have to stand up very firmly and make it clear that we do not call others inferior to ourselves and we do recognize our own failings, but we do not concede we are inferior to others and do not ignore the failings of others.

We therefore encourage the free exchange of individuals within the House of Israel: we welcome Israelis to our community and are glad to foster the settlement of Americans in the State of Israel. But the one is not a descent out of Judaism, the other not an ascent into Judaism. We recognize the many advantages to Jewish life in the State of Israel and freely concede the many problems confronting American Jewry and American Judaism. But we also see disadvantages even in Jerusalem, and advantages even in the Jewish life of Chicago or Los Angeles. Each is different from the other. No mode of Jewish living utterly solves the Jewish human problem posed by the nature of human existence. Only God will ultimately and finally solve that "problem." To allege that we stay where we are because of material considerations or that those who live in Jerusalem do so wholly through the miracles of the spirit, because they do not eat bread, is to reduce the issue to banalities. To say we cannot be "good Zionists" or the Israelis are "better Jews" is to turn into a contentious squabble what is and should remain a noble, if contested, inquiry into the most fundamental issues of the mystery of Israel's being.

12. Understanding the Other Israeli Views of Us, Our Views of Ourselves

When we speak of someone else, we talk about ourselves. How we perceive the other is a mirror of our own vision of the world. That seems to me the principal truth to guide us in trying in our setting to make sense of Zionism. I mean the setting in which, for a glorious moment after two thousand years, we stand poised between disaster and we know not what: poised for now in a condition of normality. Once, and now again, there is a place in which, if we wish to be Jews alone, that is what we may be, I mean, Israelis. There are many places in a world of freedom in which, if we wish to be many things and also Jews, that too is what we may be: Canadians and Americans, French, Argentinians. As if to perfect the matter, there is yet ample reminder of the unusual character of this moment in places in which, still and now, being a Jew is a sentence, if not of death, at least of parlous humiliation, in the Soviet Union, in Ethiopia, and also in Argentina. In all, we have the best of all times and worlds. For how long no one knows. But it need not be brief.

That is why we may stand back and ask questions about the components of this felicitous Jewish reality of the hour: how does each group relate to the other? How does each make sense of itself in what it says about the other? How, finally, does one community express its deepest concerns in what it

110

states about the other? This theme is played out in our day in the melodies of Zionism. It is because we live in a time, as I said, at which we celebrate every day of our good fortune in being contemporaries with the Jewish state. It also is because Zionism is the ineluctable metaphor of the age for all of the life, wherever it is lived, of the Jewish people. Ours is a Land-centered religion. For Scripture and Mishnah the arena of the holy is focused upon a particular place. Now whether the Land serves as a symbol only for something beyond itself and immaterial, or whether it serves for something both here and now and also in the world and time to come, or whether it serves only for something here and how, hardly matters. In fact one definitive symbol of Judaism is the Land. The additional facts that on that Land which is ours there also is a state, that that state comes into being because of the decision of nearly the whole Jewish people to build it, to populate it (for part) and to support it (for the rest)—these make this day different from all other days. They make the night which is past different from all other nights too. To me these are Zionist affirmations: the centrality of the Land in the life of the whole people, the unity of the people in its love for the Land: "We are a people, one people."

Yet Zionism stands for many things. Protean and vast, it has encompassed within its symbolic framework a wide variety of political positions, private and human aspirations. Zionism embodies a vast social change in the life of the Jewish people. It brings into being a political entity, a state, an army, a bureaucracy, out of the essentially private life of the pariah people, lacking all of these things. It is impossible to locate, in the entire history of the Jewish people, a more profound social change in the condition and being of the Jewish people than that affected, in an amazingly brief time, by the Zionist movement. Since social change is symbol change, Zionism necessarily has taken over and reshaped the entire symbolic expression of Jewry in the world as we know it. We American Jews should have to be at the outer margins of total de-Judaization to deny or defy the social changes brought about by the Zionist revolu-

tion in the life of the Jewish people and of Judaism. If we are
Zionists, as I believe we should be, it is because there is no
interesting political or existential alternative within the Jewish
frame today. As I just said, we should have to stand wholly
outside of the frame of Jewish experience and Jewish existence
to attempt a position beyond the Zionist structure, the Zionist
reading of Jewish experience and Jewish existence. Perhaps at
another time, in some other place, there was that possibility.
But here and now there is none: no choice.

But if Zionism stands for us all, still it has to stand for many
things in a Jewish world so diverse as this one. For Israelis
Zionism rightly poses and answers all Jewish questions. Its
position—that now the existence of the Jewish people has
become normal, that the Jews have reentered the life of history
expressed in socially relevant institutions and symbols of government and nationhood—addresses the everyday world. All
those Jewish realities—flag, state, people, time, place, private
and public way of life—come together into something cogent,
natural, healthy. If the world at large were cogent, natural,
healthy, Zionism would not merely proclaim how things
should be and for some now are. It also would describe how
things are for everybody: all the Jews living in one place. For
the first time since before 586 B.C.E., nearly three thousand
years of abnormality at an end. (To be sure, the meaning of the
normal and the abnormal is difficult to locate, when the state of
affairs for nearly the whole of recorded human history, so far as
Israel, the Jewish people, are concerned, is declared abnormal.) But the logic is yet there: we are a people, one people,
hence ought to live in a land and form a state.

For the Israelis, therefore, the self-evidence of the logic of the
state is called into question by the rest of the Jewish world. The
correspondence of public and private life, so whole and complete in the Jewish state, appears awry, when outside of the
Jewish state live the vast majority of the Jewish people. An
Israeli colleague told me just now, "If you are right, we are
wrong." He meant that if American Jews, in particular, turn
out to have built a stable, continuing, mature life as Jews in this

country (which then symbolizes all of the rest of the Golah), then, in his view, there was, and is, no need for a State of Israel. Either there must be a Jewish state, he argued, because one cannot live a normal and enduring life without it, therefore outside of it. Or there is no need for a Jewish state, because one can and does live a normal and enduring life outside of it. Now it is not for us to take issue on this point, because the problem captured by this view is not ours. We American Jews are not explaining ourselves when we say these words. These words do not speak for us, and they do not speak about us. We do not maintain there can be either an American Jewish community or a Jewish state, but not both. We maintain the exact opposite. There can be no American Jewish community as we now know and want that community to be, if there is no Jewish state. But if there is a Jewish state, there also is, and probably will continue to be, an American Jewish community (and so too, the rest of the Golah as well).

Why informed and thoughtful Israelis maintain the view they do—that the success of Judaism in America, the signs of stability and strength in the American Jewish community, somehow cast into doubt the basic truths of Zionism and of the Jewish state—is not difficult to explain. The Zionism regnant in the State of Israel necessarily and correctly maintains the position that the Golah is abnormal. The state is normal. I cannot imagine any other position for Israelis to take. It is natural and normal to their situation. They cannot be expected to live in a Jewish state and to imagine that doing so is not normal. The very air they breathe, the sights they see, the life they lead—these speak of what is natural and normal. It is a fact for them that to be a Jew means to live in Tel Aviv or Arad. Then it must follow, and for them it does follow, that to be a Jew does not mean to live in Southfield, Glencoe, or Larchmont. The "negation of the Golah" is not a statement of ill-will for us. It is not a negative judgment on us as human beings or even as Jews. It is a statement of fact, expressed in every breath they take and in everything they undertake to do. Nor is there anything we may say or do to call into question the very self-evidence of the "*negation* of the Golah" which forms the foundation of Israeli thinking on Zionism. Even if we fought in all their wars, by going home afterward we deny our own deeds. And we do not fight in their wars or make our livings, hence our lives, in the framework of their social and political economy.

Yet if the "negation of the Golah" forms the very foundation of the life of the state, as I believe it must, it also predisposes Israelis to notice certain things we may wish to ignore and not to place a high value on things we may think important. That is why a highly educated professor of political science, with a deep knowledge of American Jewry and profound respect for us, can maintain, "If you are right, we are wrong." It is not the sacrifice which is wrong, not the suffering, the blood of the wars, and the struggle of peacetime in a new and difficult society and economy. It is the very meaning of the sacrifice and the struggle that our very existence calls into question. Indeed, negating us and belittling our achievements form a critical component in the Israeli conception of the State of Israel.

It is no small thing, indeed, that Israelis refer to their state simply as "Israel," which, from time immemorial stood for the entire Jewish people. I believe the fathers and founders knew precisely what they wished to say when the State of Israel became straight "Israel." It was a claim of a priori legitimacy: if we are "Israel," then if you are not here, you are not "Israel," or you are less "Israel." This same view runs through the writings of Israeli philosophers of Zionism, who, quite rightly and naturally in my view, begin with the simple insistence that Zionism can never regard the life of the Golah as legitimate. They use language such as "authentic" and "inauthentic," "legitimate" and "illegitimate." I believe that the choice of these words, so fundamental in their weight, is correct.

The result will be that Israelis perceive far more rapidly than we do weaknesses both in our political situation and in our inner life as a community. Their service in this regard is heroic. They regard with contempt our institutions of Jewish expression. They dwell upon our remarkable rate of intermarriage, upon our, at best, superficial knowledge of the literature and traditions of Judaism, upon our high degree of assimilation to the prevailing society and culture of our country. They see us as much less than the Jews that they are. Within their frame of reference, they are right. The trends they perceive as dominant, trends unmodulated by any other ones, are two: political weakness, assimilation.

In the context of this discussion, the fact that these trends are real and worrisome is not important. For the issue is not what we are, but how Israelis wish to see us. There are other trends, other achievements, they do not wish to see at all. It is difficult, for example, for Israelis to take seriously the fact that American and Canadian Jews have produced a new generation of scholars in wide ranges of Jewish learning, have created a new generation of effective rabbis, have developed a new generation of efficient leaders for all sorts of Jewish purposes. They denigrate our scholarship, normally without reading it. They ridicule our rabbis, without making sense of them. They treat our leaders with disdain, without assessing their commitment and achievement. It is not because of the facts of the matter, nor even because of their high expectations which our scholars, rabbis, and leaders do not meet.

The facts do not matter. In Zionist theory there should be no signs of stability and endurance, and there are. Our community should be in an advanced state of decay and dissolution, and it is not. Our problems should represent, each of them, a crisis to life, not a chronic complaint to old age. We are not supposed to form an ongoing community, with the power to transmit to the next generation a way of being Jewish. We should not have the conceptions and modes of social organization and personal Jewish life to address the future of our own community.

Yet it is time to say the simple truth that we have found ways of being Jewish not for only one, two, or three generations, but for five or six or more. There are problems. They are real. But there also are great-grandparents who speak in perfect, unaccented American English to still-Jewish great-grandchildren.

The American Jewish community as we now know it today is stronger, better organized, and more knowledgeably Jewish than it has been at any time since the immigrants came in their masses a hundred years ago. "If you are right, we are wrong." I do not believe Zionism is wrong, in its fundamental statements, and I also do not believe Israelis are wrong, in their deepest commitments to the normal life of a Jewish state. But I do know too that we have found ways of being Jewish in the Golah for more than a few years, for more than a few individuals, and for more than a few places. I shall not apologize for saying so, since I have offered my share of criticism of our ways of carrying forward enduring ways of Jewish being. But these ways endure. They endure for most. They endure far past the immigrant generations and their children.

Since the State of Israel has flourished, now, for more than thirty years, and since the things that Zionism expected to happen—the ingathering of the exiles, the disintegration of the Golah—have not happened, we must ask ourselves why, despite these facts, the "negation of the Golah" has endured as a continuing perspective on the Golah within Israeli thought. For it is clear that the facts do not support the negation of the Golah. They suggest not only that the Golah continues and thrives as a Jewish entity. They also suggest that if Israelis affirm the Golah, they deny the state and its central propositions. We do not gain; everyone loses. Every Israeli who comes and joins our community, having grown up in a world in which immigration is a going up and emigration a going down, casts his and her vote. And it should be said, we have been vastly enriched by the settlement of Israelis in our communities, with their much greater knowledge and understanding for Judaism, the Hebrew language and literature of the Jewish people, and, it must be said, the life of the State of Israel and Zionism. For their ties to the state and its life are incomparably deeper than those of native-born American Jews. The Israelis among us form a bridge to much which we need and do not readily get; I mean, the ongoing, vigorous life of Israeli Judaism. So, as I said, "the negation of the Golah" does not find day-to-day confirmation in ordinary affairs.

I think the reason is now self-evident. A principal justification and rationalization for Zionism in its correct, Israeli formulation is the view that Zionism is the solution to "the Jewish problem," the only solution to the only problem worth discussing. Without "the negation of the Golah," fed by reports of our failures and precarious existence, much else loses meaning. The Golah must be represented as consistent, unchanging, everywhere and always the same: a bad scene for Jews. In this regard, we may profitably recall the incapacity of ancient Rome to differentiate among its barbarian enemies, either as to time or as to location and character. The enemy was always the same everywhere. In the view of Rome, "The progressive internal development of the empire took place against a backdrop that consisted of an unchangeably barbarous exterior. The never-ending savagery, deceitfulness, and turbulence of barbarians bore witness to the virtues of legally ordered society; *their existence justified the imperial regime as the hand that staved off chaos from engulfing the ordered world*" (Walter Goffart, "Rome, Constantinople, and the Barbarians," *American Historial Review* 86, 2 [April 1981], p. 280). A case may be made that the failure to differentiate among its enemies did not equip Rome to fight them intelligently and effectively. For the Romans in the end did not really know what would hit them, so to speak. A case may also be made that, in dealings with us, Israeli thinkers and leaders will do better to differentiate and seek a more nuanced view of us than they have done to date. For to persuade their own people to stay where they are, their message must be more credible than, as the facts of emigration now stand, it presently appears to be.

Twenty-five years ago Mordecai Kaplan, in *A New Zionism* (New York: Theodor Herzl Foundation, 1955), focused upon "the negation of the Golah" as a principal problem in the Zionist thought of his own time. Since Kaplan is a philosopher, he stated his judgments in terms of definitions. Thus he said, "Zionism is to be redefined, so as to assure a permanent place for Diaspora Judaism. Such a redefinition, while affirming the indispensability of *Eretz Yisrael* as the home of Judaism for Jews throughout the world, would have to stress the peoplehood, or the oneness and indivisibility, of world Jewry. On the other hand, the Jewry of Israel as nuclear to and interactive with the Jewries of the Diaspora would have to be recognized as a permanent condition." Kaplan called for a New Zionism based upon the peoplehood of all Israel and upon a new definition of Judaism. This new religion Kaplan expressed in rather banal language. It is difficult to find, in all of the literature of Jewish theology, more unappealing and even boring formulations than Kaplan gives us. The religion and mission of Israel with the new Zionism, for example, are phrased in this way: "As Zionists, we have to reconstitute our peoplehood, reclaim our ancient homeland, and revitalize our Jewish way of life. Each of these three objectives should be pursued with the end in view, both in Israel and in the Diaspora, of developing such interpersonal and intergroup relations as are likely to help us become more fully human. That is to be our religion and our mission." Now it would be fairly easy to make the case that the failure of Kaplan's New Zionism, which, in its concrete proposals, has been everywhere ignored for the last quarter-century, is based on his incapacity to write effective prose. We must never ignore, after all, the power of a well-crafted sentence. And yet I think the failure is for a different reason. No one wanted his New Zionism, because it said the wrong things to the one side, and irrelevant things to the other.

Kaplan's new Zionism—a Zionism based upon international Jewish peoplehood—really misses the point of Zionism. When we speak of Zionism, we begin with the word *Zion*, that is, we speak of a specific place. We address a set of exceedingly concrete, particular realities. When Ben-Gurion insisted that a Zionist was someone who lived in the State of Israel or who planned, in the near future, to do so, what he did was simply insist that *Zion*ism be taken seriously. His contribution, in this context, was to prevent Zionism from being made over into a rather general thing, the ethnic affirmation or assertion of Jews wherever they might be.

That other kind of Zionism—I mean, Zionism as the ethnic nationalism of the Jewish people—constitutes a danger to

Zionism because it denies Zionism's specific statements. Zionism speaks of Zion, and there is no Zion other than in Jerusalem, a real place, a real people, a real challenge to do some one thing, not many different things anywhere we want. So the New Zionism was, and is, truly incompatible with the old, not because of ill-will, nor even because of "negation of the Golah." It was and is because the New Zionism is not Zionism at all, so far as it finds the capacity to call Zionists people who do not and never will live in Zion.

Kaplan's New Zionism also was irrelevant to his American audience, and it is on this point that I wish to dwell. To state the Zionist dilemma of Amercan Jewry, we need merely learn from our Israeli colleague: "If they are right, are we wrong?" If Israelis are correct in maintaining that theirs is the authentic and legitimate way of being a Jew, that they have solved the Jewish problem, then, whether or not we are a strong and enduring community or a weak and disintegrating one, the issue is the same.

Now we cannot claim to have faced that issue, because we have been unable to do so. The reason is very simple. Faced with the views of Israeli thinkers about Jewish existence and about Zionism, we have been too Zionist ourselves to imagine that anything at all was to be said about ourselves and our existence. I do not mean to say merely that we have failed to do what we should do, for instance, counter the negation of the Golah with the affirmation of the Diaspora. No one has even wanted to do that. We are altogether too honest with ourselves. Even if we were not, we always have the example of the dull ideologues from overseas to see the flaws of so one-dimensional an argument. I mean that, living in the Zionist age, *but* in the Golah, we have preserved a seemly silence. We have pretended that the dilemmas facing us have gone away.

But they have stayed with us. We have failed to articulate a theory of ourselves within the larger Jewish world and within the broader framework of the time in which we live. In so doing, we have not expressed our Zionism; we have pretended we are not Zionists and not anything else either.

There is no Zionist theory of the Golah. We are at fault, for if such a theory of ourselves were to come forth, we are the ones to bring it forth. I for one want no part of non-Zionist theories of the Golah, let alone anti-Zionist ones. To me, as to the bulk of the Jewishly-active Jews in our community, the State of Israel is *the* Jewish state. It is all the things it claims to be. But that to me self-evident fact does not change other to me equally self-evident facts. American Jews behave as if they regard their life as Jews as authentic and legitimate. That is the case because American Jews do raise their children within a pattern of American Judaism in which they believe and which they wish to transmit to their children. The mark of what we believe to be the irreducible authenticity of our being is what we are willing to confess to our children: that above all. American Jews at home (if not when overseas) affirm the normality and self-evident correctness of their lives. We climb Massada—but we come home. We cheer everything Israeli—but we serve in our country's army and government, pay its taxes, and vote in its elections. There is no guilt I have ever located in all this. No one in our day finds it awkward or incongruous to be American and to be Jewish.

Now the counterpart to "negation of the Golah" would be a general theory of Americanism, in a Jewish modulation. That is, we should have to speak of someone else but talk about ourselves in a theory about why we are here, and *not* there. But there is no such talk. There can be none. Because we do not perceive the Israelis as they are, in all their variety and vitality, our own vision of the world is blind, without color or shadow. What I mean, then, is that for American Jewry there is no counterpart to the Zionist theory of the State of Israel, because, quite naturally, the Israelis have formed none, and because, unhappily, we have not wanted one.

And yet we do form a vast fact, we are a kind of recusant community, denying, yet not disappearing, a permanent presence in the Jewish world, powerful, attractive, successful in ways in which, within the regnant theory, we should fail. Like the recusants of British Catholicism in the seventeenth and eighteenth centuries, we will not go to the services of the other church, but we also will not go away. It does not do any good for them or for us. They are not strengthened, but we are weakened, by this failure to think about ourselves, to form a theory of what we are in the Jewish world today.

Perhaps memories of what the old and discredited "general theory of Americanism" meant for our great-grandfathers and mothers stands in the way. For, in times past, to affirm America meant to deny Judaism. In Abraham Kahan's *The Rise of David Levinsky*, we recall, as the immigrants saw the Statue of Liberty, they threw their *tefillin* into New York harbor. To be American once meant, in Jewry, to stop being a Jew. That theory has run its course. All of those persuaded by it have carried it out. There is among us no appreciable assimilationism as a regnant theory of being Jewish. Yet we must not forget that the power of Americanism, as an ideology of Jewish alternatives, far outweighed the power of Zionism when the two met head-on—I mean, in the ghetto of East European Jewry. Faced with the choice between America and Palestine, Israeli friends have told me, the idealists went to what was then Palestine, and the materialists went to America. Perhaps so, but many millions, then, walked off the map of Jewish idealism, and they did so, they told themselves, for a diversity of legitimate and honorable reasons. These reasons added up to "Americanism" as a Jewish ideology, as they added up to "Americanism" as an Armenian ideology or a German, Italian, or Chinese one. We must recall that it was only the African immigrants to America who came without free choice, hence without the need to explain to themselves what they were doing, or what was happening to them. For the rest of all our ancestors as a nation, there were reasons and explanations.

Mordecai Kaplan grasped much of this in attempting to formulate a Zionism with place for the Golah. In my view he took upon himself an impossible task. We cannot blame the intransigeance of Israeli Zionist extremists for his failure. It is not as if he was right but deprived of a hearing. Many in the State of Israel share his view of what Zionism should be, of how the state must relate to the Golah. Not a few, after all, are courteous enough to speak of us as living in the "Tefusot," in the Diaspora, rather than in Golah. But it is Golah. It remains Galut. Zionism can and must stand for all of the things in Zion: the centrality of Jerusalem, the urgency of *aliyah*, the priority of the state in the Jews' public responsibilities. I am a Zionist. I affirm these things. If my children were to settle in the State of Israel, I would affirm their choice as a Jew, even though it would be painful to me as a parent.

Yet it is time to speak about ourselves too. We live by a set of ideals and beliefs. So far we are unable to express, explain, and submit to scrutiny and criticism the things we live by. Merely because we avoid this central issue of self-analysis and self-explanation, it does not mean that problems have been solved, the difficulties of thought and theory overcome. We do not really speak of the other side. I mean, we have no theory, for ourselves, of the importance of Zionism and the State of Israel in our lives—that is, lives of self-affirming Americans and legitimate Jews.

To end where I began: We do not speak of someone else, so we fail to talk about ourselves. We do not wish to perceive the otherness of the other. So we have no mirror of our own vision of the world. We pretend that they are we, and we are they, and we all are one people. I believe that, from the perspective of the Transcendent, that is true. But since when have we asked this world to demonstrate the truths of the other? The social and political realities of the Jewish world have yet to impose themselves upon our views of the Jewish world. We know full well how our Israeli colleagues view us. So we do have the gift to see ourselves as others see us. But when shall *we* see ourselves?

Part Four

Golah and America

13. The Jewish War against the Jews

We still suffer, and always shall suffer, the wounds inflicted upon us by Hitler's war against the Jews. The murder of our people and the destruction of the great centers of its life and culture in Europe have left us weak and confused. I wish to speak about another war against the Jews, a war which goes on unabated, and which keeps us weak and confused. I refer, specifically, to the silent and subtle attack upon our being as Jews. This is an attack within the walls upon the things which make Jews Jewish. It is against the very heart and center of our life as a people, distinctive, distinct, and holy, upon this earth and within humanity.

Given the political security enjoyed by Jewry, given the high marks of commitment and devotion to "Jewish causes" exhibited by Jewry, you must wonder why I think there is an attack upon our being as Jews. If there is war, where is the blood? where are the captives and the corpses? My answer is not in the hard facts of intermarriage, the declining levels of donations to Jewish charities, the creeping disaffection with the State of Israel (without regard to a given policy), above all, the disinterest in things Jewish characteristic of at least half of our community. The war of which I speak is not fought on the frontiers of the Jewish people in this country, but in the center, at the core of its loyalist population: interested, engaged, and

125

devoted. So, once again, if there is war, where are the captives and the corpses? And who is the enemy?

First, the captive. I once had a discussion with one of my students, a Reform youth leader destined for the rabbinate, about a Hillel chaplain whose work we had both observed. I remarked that the chaplain had done a good job of organizing things but did not have Jewish "resonance," by which I meant a real feeling for Jewish ideas, Jewish books, Jewish learning. It seemed to me, I said, that the person we were discussing saw one Jewish activity as pretty much the same as any other, from dancing the hora to saying Kiddush on the Sabbath. This meant, I remarked, that we were talking about someone who did not have much of a Jewish education. And did not want one. The student replied, "Well, it depends upon what you mean by a Jewish education." When I recovered from my astonishment, I explained that by a Jewish education I meant appreciation for and knowledge of the classical tradition of Judaism, including its modern expressions of all kinds, religious and secular. And this person not only did not have such knowledge but also did not miss it. "Jewish education" is not relative; it is absolute. Knowing how to dance the hora and knowing how to say Kiddush are not of equal value. Knowing the Torah is more important than knowing the Jewish population of Cape Town, South Africa, or the history of the Jews in Sydney, Australia.

Now when I reflected on this exchange, I realized that the student with whom I had this exchange—who had, after all, studied also with me!—had never heard things I had taught. The reason is that his set of assumptions and mine were so unrelated that he did not realize he was not hearing. I did not realize he was deaf to Judaism. He is so active, engaged, and effective that I took for granted there was a generative source for the activity and engagement, a source in understanding and caring. And I was perceived by him as yet another voice among a babble of "Jewish voices," undifferentiatedly Jewish.

This is what I mean by a "captive" in the Jewish war against the Jews. I mean a child taken captive by gentiles (whether

Jewish or other), who has been raised totally alien to the ongoing and enduring teachings of Judaism. The result is that he is blameless for his unbelief. He is without guilt for his incapacity to feel and understand as a Jew. The capacity to feel and understand as a Jew, after all, is not something born into us. It is nurtured, and then, it is something we ourselves must nurture.

It indeed is hard to be a Jew, but not for the reasons people suppose. It is hard because it takes effort and work, the effort and work of learning and doing things, discipline and commitment. But our Judaism—I mean the Judaism of us Jewish Jews—demands doing only some few things. Most of these things do not lay heavy demands on the person and the way of life of the person. So here is a captive, a child taken prisoner and kept away from the true and holy life of Israel, the Jewish people. That is why, in total commitment, he could say in all sincerity, "It depends what you mean by Jewish education." Unfortunately, it does not depend. Here is one kind of victim of the Jewish war against the Jews—a good Jew, a "Jewish leader," active in all parts of campus Jewish life, indeed, the leader of a youth group and a very good one at that. Beneath the Jewish surface, behind the gossamer web of empty actions, he is at best "Jewish-style," that is, as "kosher" as a kosher-style salami sandwich.

If this is the captive, what then is the corpse of the Jewish war against the Jews? If you will grant me that there can be people who are dead in the midst of life, then the corpse of which I speak is not difficult to identify. You know that there are people who go through the motions of life but do not live. They do a job but gain nothing from their achievement. They are ascetics without a holy cause, engaged in activity without inner effect or effort. Theirs is achievement without satisfaction; donation without commitment. The best example of this kind of living dead is the one who works hard without a calling and a purpose who feels compelled to undertake Jewish activity, but who gets little from it. Examples stand ready at hand: people who go through the motions of davening but do not pray, who fill up the synagogues but do not listen when the Torah is read. Of them we know full well. But what about people who go through the motions of giving money to Jewish causes but do not fill up the synagogues and do not do those many other pleasant and enjoyable things which make being Jewish a source of joy and solace in this life?

They are, for instance, the Jews who study about Judaism in universities but do not realize that the Judaism they study also enriches the lives of the people who practice that Judaism. Just now I attended a national meeting of scholars of religion, at which scores of Jewish scholars of Judaism gave lectures. At the Friday evening minyan only a handful were present. The rest missed the beauty and the irony of that quiet hour. Then, instead of talking about Judaism, we entered the state and condition of holiness which is Judaism. And if these specialists in the study of Judaism stood apart from the practice, hence the pleasures, of Judaism, what shall we say of the cohort of people who see themselves as "Jewish leaders" by reason of the offices they hold? These are the proof that there need be no resurrection of the dead at the end of time, because, before our very eyes, the dead yet move and speak, twitch as if alive.

I mean the people who labor without love, who make things possible but do not explore the possibilities they create. They give money and work hard to support synagogues, which they do not attend; to maintain community centers, in the programs (of a Jewish character) of which they are not interested; to sustain a Jewish state they do not wish to inhabit or even visit; to make possible an entire panoply of a Jewish life they do not wish to live. What troubles me, to speak honestly and directly, is that these people have turned the being of Judaism into a set of distinct specializations. Professors learn but do not do. Rabbis give pastoral care but do not learn. "Jewish leaders" give money and hard work but do not benefit and do not participate and do not care—so their children marry out.

Everyone is special, no one is part of the average. It is through specialization that everyone is special. For if I stop being an "expert" on some part of Jewish learning, I then become merely one among other Jews, having lost my point of specialization, therefore my "right" or claim to be special. If the "big giver" joins in a minyan, he counts only for one. If the rabbi steps off his pulpit and joins in the common labor of the community, he no longer is a rabbi, but becomes an ordinary Jew. No one wants to be ordinary. So all of us preserve our specialization, doing the thing we do better than anyone else, ignoring the ways in which we in fact are not special. So that makes us what Max Weber said of the "convulsive self-importance of an age of mechanized petrification." And he says, "Of the last stage of this cultural development, it might well be truly said: 'Specialists without spirit, sensualists without heart, this nullity imagines that it has attained a level of civilization never before achieved.' " In the present context, let us say it of us all: the professors who do not profess, the rabbis who are not masters of rabbinical learning, the "Jewish leaders" who do not lead except through their money: "This nullity imagines that in America it has attained a level of Jewish civilization never before achieved."

Indeed it has. For what we have accomplished was not done to the Jewish people ever before in its history, not by the corrosive impact of modernization in the nineteenth century, not even by the murderous enemies we have survived in the twentieth century: the de-Judaization of the Jewish people by the very programs and attitudes of the most Jewish of the Jewish people, their leaders in all realms of their inner life: specialists without the Jewish spirit, sensualists with "a good Jewish heart" but with no feelings *for* Judaism at all.

Weber comments on this sort of person, which we are: "The modern man is in general, even with the best will, unable to give religious ideas a significance for culture and national character which they deserve." Now it will be asked, if this is the Jewish war against the Jews, then what is to be done to win that war?

My answer is that we must nurture in ourselves a fresh conception of who is a Jewish leader. Since it is clear that when I refer to "Jewish leader" I do not mean the people—whether rabbis, professors, or "Jewish leaders"—today cast in that role, I think the way forward is to define what we do mean, in theory, by a Jewish leader, and then proceed to apply that theory in practice. If we know what we mean by leader, then we shall recognize the leaders we do have, and we shall also know that the generals among us in fact are leading a war against us, so we are soldiers to our own destruction. What do we mean by a Jewish leader? What do we ask of a Jewish leader?

Let me first offer a definition of leadership that comes from E. M. Estes, president of General Motors Corporation—a type of position from which one would not expect the following viewpoint: "Leadership is the courage to admit mistakes, the vision to welcome change, the enthusiasm to motivate others, and the confidence to stay out of step when everyone else is marching to the wrong tune." Now whether or not that sort of leadership characterizes Mr. Estes's company and its administration I do not know. But I am fairly sure it is not a definition of leadership which applies in any way at all to the "Jewish leaders" in all their types. I know that because the principal concern of the people who today are deemed to speak for Jewry and to Jewry want anything but change, enthusiasm, confidence.

If, after all, we ask about one of the principal concerns of the "Jewish leaders" of the present time, it is with the one thing I should have expected them to deem vital to the community. The "Jewish leaders" spend their precious hours before the TV cameras and in news conferences, both in the State of Israel and in the United States, attacking what they call "dissent." Rather than arguing with those from whom they differ, the "Jewish leaders" condemn and even vilify dissenters. Indeed, the president of an Israeli university called into question what he called the "Jewish qualifications" of a principal voice of dissent. Indeed! As if any of us can or should stand in judgment upon the "Jewish qualifications" of one another!

The dissenters were told to shut up and whisper their complaints into the ears of the "leaders"—if they can get an appointment. The fact that there were, and are, serious and legitimate points of difference on objective matters of policy means nothing. "You are for us, and so you say our words in our way, when we say to say them, or you are against us, because you do not say our words in our way and when we say to say them—or because you do not say our words at all." Conformity is not to a common goal or ideal. It is to the exact words, the exact tone of voice, on that very day.

The fact that the very legitimacy of dissent within the Jewish community is called into question is profoundly troubling. The reason is twofold.

First, those who would exercise thought-control are themselves ignorant and mindless; I mean the Jewish federation and other organizational leaders who tell the Jewish intellectuals what they should and should not think as Jews.

Second, and still more troubling (for no one in fact pays attention to these "Jewish leaders"), when people wish not to argue but to suppress, it is because they are frighened. And I did not realize, and I do not think, that things are so bad for Jewry that this state of primitive terror should prevail.

On the contrary, I have far more confidence in Jewry than do the Jewish leaders who want us all to say the same thing at the same time and in the same way. But then, the "leaders" are leading the Jewish war against the Jews. And if you want to weaken the Jews, what better way do you have than to stifle dissent and drive out the dissenter? For in the consequent desert of sameness and imposed unanimity lies the death of all emotion. All commitment, all caring will perish. The one who does the job mechanically and heartlessly is the walking corpse. So in this war against fresh and different ideas and approaches to Jewry, the Jewish leaders are corpses who wish the living to become like themselves, also dead.

In conflict comes sharpening; and in difference of opinion lies vitality. In criticism, and, especially, in self-criticism, lies the chance to grow and improve. If we do nothing but defend what we have done as the best and only way of doing things, then we are not likely ever to do better than we have already done. The great forces for renewal and renaissance, the powers capable of responding to change in a changing world—these do not emerge from the ranks of those who tell us to shut up and conform. They emerge from the ranks of those willing to take risks, able to sustain criticism, and ready to recognize error and learn from error. Indeed, just as a scholar or artist or other creative person finds nourishment in learning from error, so must we all. But the route to criticism is to think freely and express possibilities without restraint. The Jewish war against the Jews will win its final victory when it persuades the Jews to stifle difference and to reject dissent. That war is very nearly won by the enemies from within, our "Jewish leaders."

Now when that war is fully won—and the day is near—then what shall we see as we gaze upon the Jewish panorama? I know the principal concern of most Jews is that there *be* Jews. "Not handing Hitler any posthumous victories" is taken to mean that we yet are here. And indeed we are. So if the impending calamity does not bring with it the total cessation of Jewish life on earth, there is apt to be a measure of comfort for most people. But that too is a measure of the nearing victory of the Jews who make war upon the Jews. So to express the full horror of the coming victory of our enemies from within the desert they are making even now, let me express something of the full sanctity of the Jewish people.

To do so, I return to that simple story about the Jewish professors, gathered in a small room, in the midst of a splendid hotel, in noise and in ordinary time and space. What did they say, and of whom did they speak? They said they are "Israel, the people God made and loves." They spoke of "the holiness of the Sabbath day and its beauty," the beauty of rest for the human person, the sanctity of renewal through the Sabbath. "Come, let us express our joy to the Lord, let us sing to the Rock of our salvation." "Come my beloved, to meet the bride." "Cause us to lie down in peace." "Blessed are you . . . who hallows the Sabbath." ". . . who has not made us like the peoples of the earth . . . who has taken delight in us." What these (sometimes) professors but (always) Jews did together was to delight in their being-together. In coming together they became holy, part of the holiness of the world's Creator and the Creator's creation.

Now to express in a simple way the opposite of that moment—the desert creeping toward us—I recall an incident of not a month ago. At a lecture at a Catholic university in Ohio, I was asked by a Jewish woman, "None of the things we care about do you seem to care about. You seem to be against us as Jews. Why in your opinion should we be Jews? And what does it mean in your opinion that we are Jews?" To this I replied very simply, "We must be Jews because God wants us to be Jews. That is how God made us, and that is what we are. We should be Jews in order to do the will of God." At this moment, a Catholic priest nearby stated very simply, "That is the only answer. That is the right answer." The stunned disbelief of the Jews in the audience hardly requires spelling out. Nothing I said for the rest of the evening made sense to them. I had closed their ears to me. But then, as I said, the Jewish war against the Jews has nearly won its final battle. When the Jews cannot understand who they are and why they are, when only a totally secular picture of themselves makes sense of themselves, and when we are able to explain ourselves only in wholly and completely this-worldly terms, then, I think, the enemy has nearly won.

For the Jewish war against the Jews is the struggle to eradicate Judaism in all its styles, expressions, and variations from the Jewish people. That is, that Judaism which speaks of Jews as Israel, the Jewish people, the holy people. It is that Judaism which imparts to the life of the holy people moments of sanctification and opportunities of joy through serving God. I speak of that Judaism which speaks of revelation and teaches revelation—I mean, the word and will of God—to this small and sacred sector of humankind. That Judaism is nearly dead. It is dead not for lack of institutions for its nurture, not for lack of protagonists for its advocacy. There are synagogues. But who has not thought that God is truly worshipped in only a few of them? The prayers are mumbled hastily in most. There are schools, but Torah is taught in only a few of them. Jewish facts and skills, the technology without the thing to be formed by the technology—these are what is taught in most. Indeed, the diminished sanctuary of Israel is what has survived this most current calamity, just as it was a diminished sanctuary which survived the first calamity, in the time of Ezekiel. And yet, what we have, we yet have. I do not criticize the synagogues, the rabbis, the schools, for all their frailty and failure. For they at least say the words which someday some may actually hear. They go through the motions which, on some occasion, some may truly do, feel, and understand.

I criticize those who constitute the vast majority of Jewish Jewry, who treat the synagogue as a curious survival if they are members, and who ignore the synagogue entirely if they are not.

I condemn the vast majority of Jewry, who do not realize that rabbis in general know things worth knowing, teach things of a complete authenticity to the Torah of Israel and the will of the God of Israel.

I reject the complacent atheism of the Jewish people of our day and place. I abhor the comfortable assumption that, of course, there is no God, there is no issue of revelation, there is no problem of redemption.

I stand against the self-evidence of the secular. I speak for the inexorable, the inescapable, the indelible stigmata of our enduring sanctification.

We are what we are—I mean, we are Jews—because God loves us. God loves us not because we are mighty or wise or important in this world. God loves us not because we have done things to make God love us. God loves us because of where we come from, where we are going, and what we were and again can be. God loves us, indeed, even in this unredeemed and disappointing world of ours, because of what some Jews even today are.

There are heroes of the Jewish spirit among us. These are the enemies against whom the Jewish war against the Jews is to be fought.

I do not know who those heroes are—and would not name them if I knew. None of us may claim to be a hero in the struggle against the Jewish war against the Jews. On the contrary, it is only when we recognize that there is a war to be resisted that we understand we have the chance at heroism. There is much to be said about the victims of the war. But none of us should attempt to specify the forces yet sustaining the sanctity of Israel, the Jewish people. Indeed, the mystery of our day is that the sanctity of Israel, the Jewish people, yet endures, despite it all, against it all. And yet it does. And that sanctity is yet at hand to all who wish to enter into it, to shape and reshape their lives in response to the holiness of the Jewish people, of the Torah, of the Sabbath, of the life of prayer, learning, and inner renewal.

I know full well that I will be heard to preach a kind of "Jewish fundamentalism," even a kind of "Orthodoxy." I do not mind. For I do believe that there really are within the Orthodox sector of the Jewish people important minds and hearts, which both grasp and are able to convey the meaning of the sanctification of the Jewish people. But since I also am entirely certain that within all sectors of the Jewish people are to be discovered minds and hearts capable of grasping and conveying to us that power of holiness enduring within our very being, I cannot be dismissed as "merely" Orthodox (even though I should be proud to have my lot among them).

But to understand the sanctification of Israel, the Jewish people, we have to remember that all Israel is holy, and that the power and force of sanctification is within all born of the seed of Abraham or called to the faith and Torah of Moses. So it is not possible to imagine that any child of Israel, the Jewish people, stands further than another from the Holy One of Israel or nearer than another to the sanctifying, holy life of Israel. Do not, then, ask me where to find the place of Israel's sanctification. It is within us all.

What has all of this got to do with Golah and Galut? One mark of Galut—of being out of place—is the self-hatred of Jews who reject or resent their Jewishness. The resentment indicates unhappiness at the difference that makes us Jews and not something—anything—else. We feel different because we are in Golah. We cannot expect the difference to go away until we go somewhere else. So Galut is a function of Golah. As a Zionist, I must see Golah for what it is.

But as a Jew, possessed of that long memory I mentioned in the opening paper, I also know that this is how things have been for a very long time. For the one extreme Golah is realized in the Shoah, an ever-present possibility on the face of the earth, not only for Jews of the Golah, not alone for the entire Jewish people, but for all humankind. The other extreme of Golah is realized in Torah, also an eternal possibility for Israel, the Jewish people, among all humankind. The soul of Israel frames the battlefields of the Jewish war against the Jews. It also is the prize. The Jewish war for the Jews is fought in the wars of Torah. In our struggles, especially in the strife within our own divided hearts, we find contemporary meanings of Golah and Shoah, but also of Torah.

Part Five

Epilogue

14. Where Do We Go from Here? Jewish Identity in the Twenty-first Century

When we ask, "Who is a Jew?" we all know the answer. A Jew is the offspring of a Jewish mother (for the Reform and Reconstructionist: a Jewish parent). Since that obvious answer eludes no one, the question clearly means to raise a different sort of issue altogether. It addresses the more profound question of what it means to be a Jew, to which answers do not appear to be altogether self-evident at all. For when we ask questions of meaning, we immediately introduce considerations of context and circumstance. And then matters become truly complicated.

The circumstance is twofold: the Golah or the State of Israel? The context is still more diverse: man or woman, rich or poor, religious or secular, and, if religious, of what tradition, and, if secular, with what consequence? But even if we could all agree that in a given context, the range of choices still may be limited to a few, we have yet to introduce the still more complicating factor of the historical setting. When we ask the question dictates as many limits on the possible answers as to whom we address the question. Clearly, simple logic requires us to select, for a point of entry into the question, some few considerations among many entirely valid and appropriate ones. Even here, however, the order in which we take up our program of differentiation—whether geographic, political, social, economic, religious, or gender—will also govern the range of possibilities as we proceed down our list.

If then I may select the single most significant point of differentiation, one which takes pride of place before all others, it has to be the age in which we live. When we make our lives— the larger situation in world-history—dictates all the other choices that we make. A moment's reflection will show that if we were asking who is a Jew in the eighteenth century, the possible answers, proposed by the political climate of the age, would vastly differ from those among which we today may choose. So before we reach the issue of either the social entity or the individual component—the nation, the self—we have to begin with the setting that encompasses us all. We face the end of the twentieth century.

Looking ahead, what choices fall open, and what turn out to be closed off, by the condition of world civilization at the end of this most difficult century in the history of the Jewish people— difficult but also triumphant? In a world of nation-states, we are privileged to witness, and some of us are privileged to participate in, the building of the Jewish state. In an age of total war Jews wherever they live share in the tragedy of a world of continuous battle. In a time of uncertainty and deep despair about the future of humanity, we Jews too contemplate the radical choice of being or extinction. Yet the choice does not encompass the nation, not at all. Short of nuclear catastrophe, the Jews as a nation in the State of Israel and as a clearly defined social entity in the democratic countries of the Golah will endure. The individual may imagine defining a Jewish identity. But no individual in our day will decide whether or not the Jewish nation dies or lives. That issue was settled by the creation of the State of Israel, on the one side, and by the collective decision of the Golah Jewries to carry on their group life beyond the Shoah, on the other. Indeed, the issue never could have been in doubt.

Yet once we recognize that, come what may, so long as humanity endures, the Jewish people will proceed on through time and change, we recognize the narrow limitations within

which Jewish individuals make choices. They will not deter-
mine whether or not the people continues to live, but they will
decide what kind of people the Jews will constitute: how many
or how few, how distinctive or how trivial and petty the
definitive difference. Jewish individuals who treat "being Jewish" as peripheral to their lives in the Golah will transform the
Jewish group into something casual and lacking all influence
and cohesion. In the State of Israel they will transform the
Jewish state into something routine and commonplace among
nations. Jewish individuals who persist in the trend not to
reproduce themselves will make certain that, in the Golah, the
Jews dwindle in numbers and in consequence, and, in the State
of Israel, in power and importance.

True enough, there is an absolute number that a group
requires to sustain itself. Even though in most of the Golah
communities we do not reach that number at which an irre-
versible decline begins, we must recognize that the vitality,
diversity, and promise of our community, to begin with, depend upon ample numbers to explore and sustain a broad
range of possibilities. Without sufficient numbers of Jews, there
can be nothing Jewish. What constitutes a sufficient population
we do not know. But in the next two or three decades, of which
we speak, we are not apt to find out, and, in the State of Israel,
much longer than that. So whatever we make of our "being
Jewish," we may be certain that we decide mainly for ourselves. No private person is going to answer for the Jewish
nation as a whole the question, to be or not to be. Nor will any
gentile. Being or extinction: the issue depends upon humanity
as a whole. But within the polity of peoples, we face no more,
or no fewer, risks than anyone else.

Three issues seem to me critical to the definition of the
Jewish situation in the Golah in the next decades: gender, class,
and culture. For when we today ask, "Who is a Jew?" the
answer does not fall solely within the limit of the status of the
mother or the parent. Today people pretty much take for
granted that if you are male, rich, and at most formally religious, you are somehow more Jewish, that is, more normal,

than if you are female, poor, and either intensely religious or quite secular but Jewish in some other than religious mode. The benign consensus treats as normal the wealthy Jewish male who attends the synagogue a few times a year but does not take those matters very seriously. He spends much more time in matters of politics than religion, fund-raising than culture, action than reflection. When women achieve recognition, it is within the male pattern. When the poor find their place in the scheme of things, it is within the definitions already laid down by the wealthy Jews. When the secular but very Jewish, on the one side, and the intensely religious (Judaic), on the other, try to find their way into the Jewish consensus, it is at the cost of their deepest convictions. Or they pay a heavy price in duplicity.

The principal activities that occupy the Golah communities so define modes of Jewish identification as to foster the pattern just now outlined. The Jews begin Jewish activity with an interest in two things, both of them practical: raising money, exercising political influence in public life. Both activities, for the Golah, focus, as is quite natural, on the State of Israel. But the definition of the good Jew of the Golah by reference to pro-Israelism hardly qualifies as a Zionist definition of who is a Jew. For (to use the cultic phrase) "the centrality of Jerusalem" would surprise the Golah Jews if it were presented to them as a practical program. They do not plan to go there. Nor does what actually happens in the Jewish state occupy much attention, except in two aspects: foreign policy and philanthropy. Jews care intensely about what is good for the State of Israel—but they do not want to live there. They genuinely concern themselves with welfare programs for the needy of the Jewish state—but they do not plan personally to help build an economy and a society to solve the problems of poverty and inequality. So the practical definition of what it means to be a Jew—money and politics—governs what will matter when the Golah Jews reflect on what they owe, and do not owe, to the Jewish state too.

What have gender, class, and culture to do with the exercise of power? To ask the question is to answer it. Power, in the form of politics or philanthropy, is what men do. Women take an auxiliary role, except when they can define themselves in the normal, that is, the male, framework. Accordingly, we do not even know what being Jewish would consist of if women were to impose their values, their most profound concerns, upon the framing of the Jewish agenda. Along these same lines, the rich have power, the poor do not. The rich matter, the poor scarcely count. If, then, we define the important Jewish activities around fund-raising and political action, we by definition direct to the rear people whose gifts do not encompass the capacity to make (or, as is now common, inherit) a lot of money. When the people in control define what is important by reference to what they control, then other sorts of capacities prove without value. So the gifts of sensibility and intelligence, the capacity to reason and to understand, the power to perceive and to clarify—gifts widely diffused among the population, not commanded solely by those with money—turn out to be null. That is why the Jewish community of the Golah is run by lawyers and businessmen. That is why no place awaits people who are not lawyers and not businessmen, unless they accept their values and can do or at least admire the things they do.

The matter of culture proves more complex than the others, because when we speak of intellect and sensibility, taste and judgment move to the fore, the things to be weighed and measured and counted move to the side. But who can weigh intelligence, measure sensibility, or assess the value of commitment? In this regard, as in many others, life in the State of Israel indeed turns out to be more normal than life in the Golah. There the gifts of leadership, courage, perseverance, and commitment, the capacity of give oneself and one's talents of heart and mind—these matter. For in the building of a nation, a government and army, a society, the power to lead and the capacity to set an example of human greatness count. In the truncated and only partial life of the Jewish world of the Golah, lived in fewer dimensions and in smaller ways than the full and complete life of the Jewish world of the Jewish state, there is little space for largeness of spirit. To the contrary, to be a Jew finds definition in only a few, limited ways, with the consequence that only some things truly count, mainly practical, mostly external to the inner life of the individual human being.

It is no more normal, within the definition of Jewish identity in the Golah, to be intensely religious than it is to be militantly secular. Both sorts of Jews may add up to sizable numbers, but count for nought. It is not that the appeal of religious commitment ("fanaticism") bears no resonance, or that deep ethnic loyalty ("Jewishness") not infused with religious conviction characterizes few. The contrary is the case. Large numbers of Jews in the Golah hold the view that only through total separation from the gentile world on religious grounds and through sacred disciplines will the Jews endure, and, I hasten to add, these same Jews maintain that that is precisely how God wants the Jews to live.

Still larger numbers of Golah Jews maintain a deep loyalty to the Jewish people but do not endow that sentiment with religious valence of any kind. To them the Jews form an ethnic community. They cherish the customs and ceremonies of that ethnic group, including the concern for the State of Israel. But none of these distinctive practices and beliefs constitutes more than a this-worldly social and cultural activity and viewpoint.

Whether the fanatically religious or the militantly ethnic, these sorts of Jews play no major role in the definition of what will constitute the legitimate and important dimensions of being Jewish. The broad consensus, framed by the male, the rich, the practical, takes slight note of the aberrations of excessive conviction or improper conviction. The consensus that tells us what ordinary people who are Jews must be holds that golden mean: Jewish, but not too Jewish. That is to say, we are not supposed to be so Jewish that we cannot find our place within the accepted consensus of our nation. In the third generation of American Jews, what that meant was that we should be Jewish, but not so Jewish that we might not find our rightful place as undifferentiated Americans too. For the fourth generation the same view then excludes those Jews who wish to be so Jewish that they will serve God, who loves them. It also excludes those Jews who wish to be Jewish in other ways, along other lines, than the accepted ones.

The benign consensus works, but not too well for three reasons.

First, it excludes the somewhat more than 50 percent of Jews who are women. Whatever matters to the Jewish woman as a woman, when she thinks through what her gender dictates as important about the Jewish tradition, no one yet knows. We are still in the beginnings of the struggle for complete equality of position and right of free expression for women in Jewry.

Second, it excludes the somewhat more than 70 or 80 percent or more of Jews, men and women, who are not rich enough to make noteworthy financial contributions to the fund-raising programs of Jewry. (I suspect the proportion is far higher, since my friends in the fund-raising world tell me the one who can give less than $10,000 really cannot make much of a difference, except in morale.)

Third, and most important, it excludes that minority that believes too much or cares too deeply: the contentious, the committed, and the ones who bear too heavy a burden of conviction. The Jews who hear God speak to them when they study Torah, the Jews who find speaking the Yiddish or the Hebrew language a moment of full Jewish expression (whatever they say in those languages)—these and the many who are like them in diverse modes of human expression find no hearing in Jewry at large. True, the intellectuals enjoy attention. But it is only when they say what people want to hear, paint what people can understand, without effort, as "Jewish," compose what people can hear, without education, as "Jewish," portray the Jewish past and present in ways people can accept without pain. That is why Jewish education makes little room for the intellect and consists, in the main, of an exercise in indoctrination in a resentful ideology of blood and peoplehood. That is why Jewish scholarship turns into mere fact-mongering, with the facts so arranged as to produce the illusion of learning. Once scholarship probes into the deeper layers of meaning, raises up for discussion questions of why and wherefore, not merely how, where, and when, scholarship loses all power to attract.

So, in all, there is a rather coarse and material veneer to the modes of definition of worthwhile Jewish activity, normal Jewish identity, in the Golah. An ideology of blood and peoplehood, of survival for the sake of survival, raises barriers to the exploration of Jewish sensibility and feeling, to the inquiry into truth and right, that are supposed to define worthwhile life as a Jew. A stress on politics and philanthropy for a faraway cause—a State of Israel everyone cherishes and no one wants to see too clearly or close-up—distorts and demeans Jewish humanity. For politics translates what matters into votes and influence, as much as philanthropy, pursued without a higher motivation, transforms all matters of value into the measure of material wealth. In these two ways, then, individuality gives way to what is to be exchanged in an impersonal way, and everyone conforms by losing all distinctive traits of identification. Then Jewish identification loses touch with the individual character, the humanity of Jews, since what we give is only the same thing, whether votes or dollars or even an occasional pilgrimage to Israeli hotels.

To the creation of the program of sameness and action of a rather common sort, the State of Israel makes no important contribution. We of the Golah have done it all ourselves. For the Israelis continue to insist they want us more than they want our money or even our political influence (such as it is). So they would define the good Jew of the Golah in a way quite different from the present definition. It would address itself, after all, to human choice, to what makes this one better than that through what one does and the other does not do. The prospective *oleh* is better than the rest of the Jews, within such a definition of Jewish identity. That means, at a very minimum, that something about the person other than wealth or influence or knowhow marks that person as more authentic, more of a model for others, than anyone else. But in our system of Jewish identification, nothing much matters except for those material deeds everyone is supposed to do, indifferently and equally.

At the same time we have to recognize that the Golah communities have come a long way in the past three decades. In the years after World War II the Golah communities focused their ideal on the creation of a nonsectarian community at home, alongside nonsectarian "relief activities" overseas. The Jewish organizations and institutions that marked the Jew as different enjoyed considerably less support and standing than did those aimed at minimizing difference. In a practical way a policy of indifference to Jewish education and culture aimed at the effective de-Judaization of the Jews of the Golah.

Today, by contrast, no responsible Jewish leader advocates assimilation of Jews into some common mass of society. The central Jewish community agencies focus their best efforts on fostering Jewish distinctiveness. So we have much of which to be proud. But what makes the Jews different from others? That, as I have argued, presents its problems. If what makes us different from others is not what we do, but merely for what we do it, then we are not going to endure as an interesting and important group. If we define ourselves by neutral actions, in no way special to ourselves and expressive of our deeply felt human convictions about the worth of life, then these neutral actions will accomplish unimportant things. And that is the case, even though the actions themselves aim at accomplishing particular and Jewish ends. What seems to me to present us with the key to a vast reform of the Golah communities is a reconsideration of three matters.

We have to define the Jew in such a way that the woman is normal as much as the man, that the poor person matters as much as the rich, and that the one of deep enthusiasms and convictions—whether about God or about peoplehood—belongs as much as the amiable and the agreeable, the tolerant and the tolerable. If the Jew today is a rich man who writes a check for a Jewish cause in which he participates only in a desultory way, the Jew tomorrow should be the woman or the man who personally participates in distinctively substantive Jewish works: learning, living, loving, and laboring as a Jew, whatever, in context, that must mean.

Index

Holocaust attitudes, 58-68, 70-71
Jewish State: *see* State of Israel
Jewish studies, 45, 80
Jewish Theological Seminary, 104
Judaism: and American Jewry, 113-,
120-121; American Jewry and Zionism, 79-87, 119; Babylonian Talmud, law of Judaism, 3-5; exile
and Jewishness, 1-9, 21-30; Jewish
culture, 32-36; Jewish education,
126-135; Jewish experience and
way of life, 42-48; Jewishness in
exile, 14-17; post-Holocaust attitudes, 60-61

Kaplan, Mordecai, 82, 117-119, 121

Lewis, Sinclair, 27

Messianic hope, 3, 74; 1967 fervor,
61-62
Mishnah, theology of, 3-5

National Jewish Post, 100
Nazism, Holocaust and redemption,
51-76

Orthodox Judaism, 104

Politics: and American Jewry, 45-46;
Golah Jewry, 142

Rawidowicz, Simon, 41, 43-44, 47-48
Reform Judaism, 104

Sachar, Howard, 100
Shoah: see Holocaust

"Shoah, Incorporated," 52
South Africa, Jewish community life,
39-42
State of Israel: American Jewry, relation with, 88-99; American Zionism, 79-87, 119; attitudes toward,
125; contributing to Golah, 116-
117; ending Galut, 21-30; Holocaust and redemption, 51-76, 103;
Jewish studies, 45; population
changes, 42, 44; relationship with
Jewish communities, 37-40, 112-
122; Zionism and Golah, 1-9
Steiner, George, 51
Szold, Henrietta, 83

Tchernichovsky, 44
Torah life in exile, 1-3, 6

United Jewish Appeal, 13, 106

Wars of: 1967, 61, 63; 1973, 63
Weber, Max, 129
Women and American Jewry, 145
World Zionist Congress, 82, 88

Yadin, Yigael, 106

Zionism: American Jewry, 13, 78-87,
119; analysis of, 11-122; in Golah,
1-9; Holocaust and State of Israel,
52-76; New Zionism and Diaspora
Judaism, 117-119; post-Holocaust
attitudes, 64; relation of American
Jewry and State of Israel, 8, 13,
105-109, 119